# ULTIMATE EXERCISE

## DIARY FOR THE BRIGHT & BUDDING ATHLETE

Activinotes

*Activinotes*

DAILY JOURNALS, PLANNERS, NOTEBOOKS AND OTHER BLANK BOOKS

Copyright 2016

# THIS BOOK BELONGS

# TO

_____

# This Weeks

# Workout

- Record Your Weekly Workout

- Record Your Daily Workout

- Record Calories Burned

# DAILY LOG

| DATE: | | | Su M Tu W Th F Sa | |
| --- | --- | --- | --- | --- |
| TIME | QTY | FOOD | CALORIES | FAT |
| | | | | |
| | | | | |
| | | | | |
| | | | | |
| | | | | |
| | | | | |
| | | | | |
| | | | | |
| | | | | |
| | | | | |
| | | | | |
| | | | | |
| | | | | |
| | | | | |
| | | | | |
| | | | | |
| | | | | |
| | | | | |
| | | | | |
| | | | | |
| | | | | |
| | | | | |
| | | | | |
| | | | | |
| | | | | |

# WORK IT OUT

| WORKOUT | TIME | DURATION | CALORIES BURNED |
|---------|------|----------|-----------------|
| _____ | _____ | _____ | _____ |
| _____ | _____ | _____ | _____ |
| _____ | _____ | _____ | _____ |

WATER
(8-12 GLASSES PER DAY

◯ ◯ ◯ ◯ ◯ ◯ ◯
◯ ◯ ◯ ◯ ◯ ◯ ◯

| WORKOUT | TIME | DURATION | CALORIES BURNED |
|---------|------|----------|-----------------|
| _____ | _____ | _____ | _____ |
| _____ | _____ | _____ | _____ |
| _____ | _____ | _____ | _____ |

WATER
(8-12 GLASSES PER DAY

◯ ◯ ◯ ◯ ◯ ◯ ◯
◯ ◯ ◯ ◯ ◯ ◯ ◯

| WORKOUT | TIME | DURATION | CALORIES BURNED |
|---------|------|----------|-----------------|
| _____ | _____ | _____ | _____ |
| _____ | _____ | _____ | _____ |
| _____ | _____ | _____ | _____ |

WATER
(8-12 GLASSES PER DAY

◯ ◯ ◯ ◯ ◯ ◯ ◯
◯ ◯ ◯ ◯ ◯ ◯ ◯

REMARKS:

# WORK IT OUT

| WORKOUT | TIME | DURATION | CALORIES BURNED |
|---------|------|----------|-----------------|
| _____ | _____ | _____ | _____ |
| _____ | _____ | _____ | _____ |
| _____ | _____ | _____ | _____ |

WATER
(8-12 GLASSES PER DAY

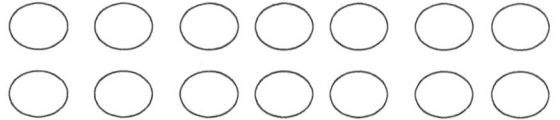

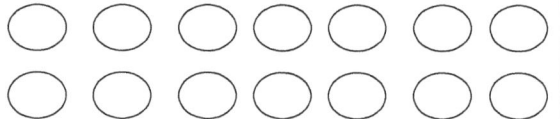

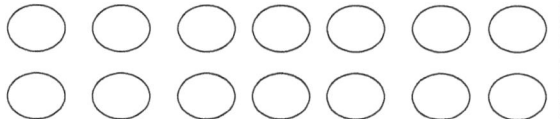

○ ○ ○ ○ ○ ○ ○
○ ○ ○ ○ ○ ○ ○

| WORKOUT | TIME | DURATION | CALORIES BURNED |
|---------|------|----------|-----------------|
| _____ | _____ | _____ | _____ |
| _____ | _____ | _____ | _____ |
| _____ | _____ | _____ | _____ |

WATER
(8-12 GLASSES PER DAY

○ ○ ○ ○ ○ ○ ○
○ ○ ○ ○ ○ ○ ○

| WORKOUT | TIME | DURATION | CALORIES BURNED |
|---------|------|----------|-----------------|
| _____ | _____ | _____ | _____ |
| _____ | _____ | _____ | _____ |
| _____ | _____ | _____ | _____ |

WATER
(8-12 GLASSES PER DAY

○ ○ ○ ○ ○ ○ ○
○ ○ ○ ○ ○ ○ ○

REMARKS:

# WORK IT OUT

| WORKOUT | TIME | DURATION | CALORIES BURNED |
|---------|------|----------|-----------------|
| _____ | _____ | _____ | _____ |
| _____ | _____ | _____ | _____ |
| _____ | _____ | _____ | _____ |

WATER
(8-12 GLASSES PER DAY

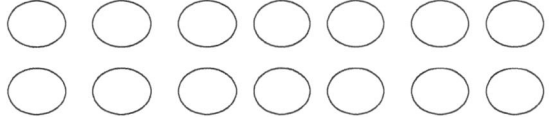

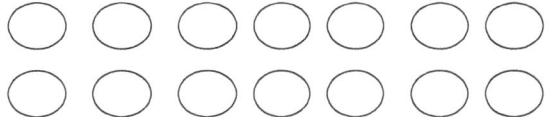

◯ ◯ ◯ ◯ ◯ ◯ ◯
◯ ◯ ◯ ◯ ◯ ◯ ◯

| WORKOUT | TIME | DURATION | CALORIES BURNED |
|---------|------|----------|-----------------|
| _____ | _____ | _____ | _____ |
| _____ | _____ | _____ | _____ |
| _____ | _____ | _____ | _____ |

WATER
(8-12 GLASSES PER DAY

◯ ◯ ◯ ◯ ◯ ◯ ◯
◯ ◯ ◯ ◯ ◯ ◯ ◯

| WORKOUT | TIME | DURATION | CALORIES BURNED |
|---------|------|----------|-----------------|
| _____ | _____ | _____ | _____ |
| _____ | _____ | _____ | _____ |

WATER
(8-12 GLASSES PER DAY

◯ ◯ ◯ ◯ ◯ ◯ ◯
◯ ◯ ◯ ◯ ◯ ◯ ◯

REMARKS:

# WORK IT OUT

| WORKOUT | TIME | DURATION | CALORIES BURNED |
|---------|------|----------|-----------------|
| _____ | _____ | _____ | _____ |
| _____ | _____ | _____ | _____ |
| _____ | _____ | _____ | _____ |

WATER
(8-12 GLASSES PER DAY

◯ ◯ ◯ ◯ ◯ ◯ ◯
◯ ◯ ◯ ◯ ◯ ◯

| WORKOUT | TIME | DURATION | CALORIES BURNED |
|---------|------|----------|-----------------|
| _____ | _____ | _____ | _____ |
| _____ | _____ | _____ | _____ |
| _____ | _____ | _____ | _____ |

WATER
(8-12 GLASSES PER DAY

◯ ◯ ◯ ◯ ◯ ◯ ◯
◯ ◯ ◯ ◯ ◯ ◯

| WORKOUT | TIME | DURATION | CALORIES BURNED |
|---------|------|----------|-----------------|
| _____ | _____ | _____ | _____ |
| _____ | _____ | _____ | _____ |
| _____ | _____ | _____ | _____ |

WATER
(8-12 GLASSES PER DAY

◯ ◯ ◯ ◯ ◯ ◯ ◯
◯ ◯ ◯ ◯ ◯ ◯

REMARKS:

# WORK IT OUT

| WORKOUT | TIME | DURATION | CALORIES BURNED |
|---|---|---|---|
| _____ | _____ | _____ | _____ |
| _____ | _____ | _____ | _____ |
| _____ | _____ | _____ | _____ |

WATER
(8-12 GLASSES PER DAY

◯ ◯ ◯ ◯ ◯ ◯ ◯
◯ ◯ ◯ ◯ ◯ ◯ ◯

| WORKOUT | TIME | DURATION | CALORIES BURNED |
|---|---|---|---|
| _____ | _____ | _____ | _____ |
| _____ | _____ | _____ | _____ |
| _____ | _____ | _____ | _____ |

WATER
(8-12 GLASSES PER DAY

◯ ◯ ◯ ◯ ◯ ◯ ◯
◯ ◯ ◯ ◯ ◯ ◯ ◯

| WORKOUT | TIME | DURATION | CALORIES BURNED |
|---|---|---|---|
| _____ | _____ | _____ | _____ |
| _____ | _____ | _____ | _____ |
| _____ | _____ | _____ | _____ |

WATER
(8-12 GLASSES PER DAY

◯ ◯ ◯ ◯ ◯ ◯ ◯
◯ ◯ ◯ ◯ ◯ ◯ ◯

REMARKS:

# WORK IT OUT

| WORKOUT | TIME | DURATION | CALORIES BURNED |
|---------|------|----------|-----------------|
| _____ | _____ | _____ | _____ |
| _____ | _____ | _____ | _____ |
| _____ | _____ | _____ | _____ |

WATER
(8-12 GLASSES PER DAY

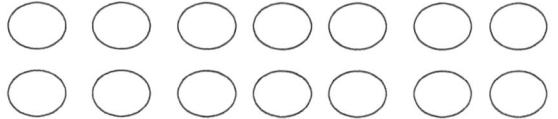

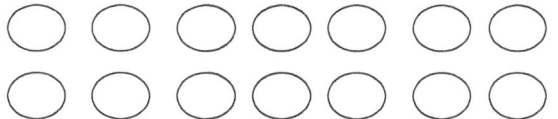

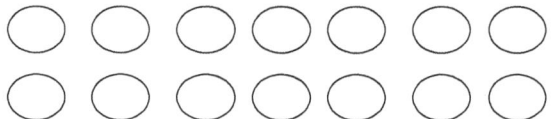

◯ ◯ ◯ ◯ ◯ ◯ ◯
◯ ◯ ◯ ◯ ◯ ◯ ◯

| WORKOUT | TIME | DURATION | CALORIES BURNED |
|---------|------|----------|-----------------|
| _____ | _____ | _____ | _____ |
| _____ | _____ | _____ | _____ |
| _____ | _____ | _____ | _____ |

WATER
(8-12 GLASSES PER DAY

◯ ◯ ◯ ◯ ◯ ◯ ◯
◯ ◯ ◯ ◯ ◯ ◯ ◯

| WORKOUT | TIME | DURATION | CALORIES BURNED |
|---------|------|----------|-----------------|
| _____ | _____ | _____ | _____ |
| _____ | _____ | _____ | _____ |
| _____ | _____ | _____ | _____ |

WATER
(8-12 GLASSES PER DAY

◯ ◯ ◯ ◯ ◯ ◯ ◯
◯ ◯ ◯ ◯ ◯ ◯ ◯

REMARKS:

# WORK IT OUT

| WORKOUT | TIME | DURATION | CALORIES BURNED |
|---------|------|----------|-----------------|
| _____ | _____ | _____ | _____ |
| _____ | _____ | _____ | _____ |
| _____ | _____ | _____ | _____ |

WATER
(8-12 GLASSES PER DAY

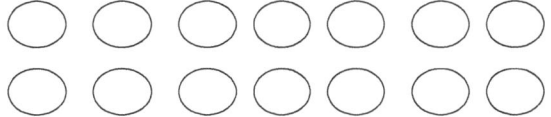

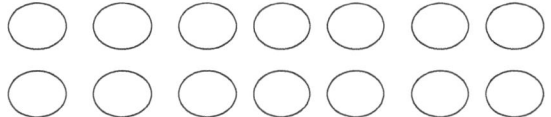

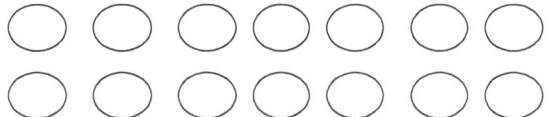

◯ ◯ ◯ ◯ ◯ ◯ ◯
◯ ◯ ◯ ◯ ◯ ◯ ◯

| WORKOUT | TIME | DURATION | CALORIES BURNED |
|---------|------|----------|-----------------|
| _____ | _____ | _____ | _____ |
| _____ | _____ | _____ | _____ |
| _____ | _____ | _____ | _____ |

WATER
(8-12 GLASSES PER DAY

◯ ◯ ◯ ◯ ◯ ◯ ◯
◯ ◯ ◯ ◯ ◯ ◯ ◯

| WORKOUT | TIME | DURATION | CALORIES BURNED |
|---------|------|----------|-----------------|
| _____ | _____ | _____ | _____ |
| _____ | _____ | _____ | _____ |
| _____ | _____ | _____ | _____ |

WATER
(8-12 GLASSES PER DAY

◯ ◯ ◯ ◯ ◯ ◯ ◯
◯ ◯ ◯ ◯ ◯ ◯ ◯

REMARKS:

# EXERCISE LOG

| DATE: | Su M Tu W Th F Sa |
|-------|-------------------|

| EXERCISES | SETS | TIME |
|-----------|------|------|
|  |  |  |
|  |  |  |
|  |  |  |
|  |  |  |
|  |  |  |
|  |  |  |
|  |  |  |
|  |  |  |
|  |  |  |
|  |  |  |
|  |  |  |
|  |  |  |
|  |  |  |

# This Weeks

# Workout

- Record Your Weekly Workout

- Record Your Daily Workout

- Record Calories Burned

# DAILY LOG

| | | DATE: | | | Su M Tu W Th F Sa | |
|---|---|---|---|---|---|---|

| TIME | QTY | FOOD | CALORIES | FAT |
|---|---|---|---|---|
| | | | | |
| | | | | |
| | | | | |
| | | | | |
| | | | | |
| | | | | |
| | | | | |
| | | | | |
| | | | | |
| | | | | |
| | | | | |
| | | | | |
| | | | | |
| | | | | |
| | | | | |
| | | | | |
| | | | | |
| | | | | |
| | | | | |
| | | | | |
| | | | | |
| | | | | |
| | | | | |
| | | | | |
| | | | | |

# WORK IT OUT

| WORKOUT | TIME | DURATION | CALORIES BURNED |
|---------|------|----------|-----------------|
| _____ | _____ | _____ | _____ |
| _____ | _____ | _____ | _____ |
| _____ | _____ | _____ | _____ |

WATER
(8-12 GLASSES PER DAY        ◯ ◯ ◯ ◯ ◯ ◯ ◯
                             ◯ ◯ ◯ ◯ ◯ ◯ ◯

| WORKOUT | TIME | DURATION | CALORIES BURNED |
|---------|------|----------|-----------------|
| _____ | _____ | _____ | _____ |
| _____ | _____ | _____ | _____ |
| _____ | _____ | _____ | _____ |

WATER
(8-12 GLASSES PER DAY        ◯ ◯ ◯ ◯ ◯ ◯ ◯
                             ◯ ◯ ◯ ◯ ◯ ◯ ◯

| WORKOUT | TIME | DURATION | CALORIES BURNED |
|---------|------|----------|-----------------|
| _____ | _____ | _____ | _____ |
| _____ | _____ | _____ | _____ |
| _____ | _____ | _____ | _____ |

WATER
(8-12 GLASSES PER DAY        ◯ ◯ ◯ ◯ ◯ ◯ ◯
                             ◯ ◯ ◯ ◯ ◯ ◯ ◯

REMARKS:

# WORK IT OUT

| WORKOUT | TIME | DURATION | CALORIES BURNED |
|---------|------|----------|-----------------|
| _____ | _____ | _____ | _____ |
| _____ | _____ | _____ | _____ |
| _____ | _____ | _____ | _____ |

WATER
(8-12 GLASSES PER DAY

◯ ◯ ◯ ◯ ◯ ◯ ◯
◯ ◯ ◯ ◯ ◯ ◯ ◯

| WORKOUT | TIME | DURATION | CALORIES BURNED |
|---------|------|----------|-----------------|
| _____ | _____ | _____ | _____ |
| _____ | _____ | _____ | _____ |
| _____ | _____ | _____ | _____ |

WATER
(8-12 GLASSES PER DAY

◯ ◯ ◯ ◯ ◯ ◯ ◯
◯ ◯ ◯ ◯ ◯ ◯ ◯

| WORKOUT | TIME | DURATION | CALORIES BURNED |
|---------|------|----------|-----------------|
| _____ | _____ | _____ | _____ |
| _____ | _____ | _____ | _____ |
| _____ | _____ | _____ | _____ |

WATER
(8-12 GLASSES PER DAY

◯ ◯ ◯ ◯ ◯ ◯ ◯
◯ ◯ ◯ ◯ ◯ ◯ ◯

REMARKS:

# WORK IT OUT

| WORKOUT | TIME | DURATION | CALORIES BURNED |
|---------|------|----------|-----------------|
| _____ | _____ | _____ | _____ |
| _____ | _____ | _____ | _____ |
| _____ | _____ | _____ | _____ |

WATER
(8-12 GLASSES PER DAY

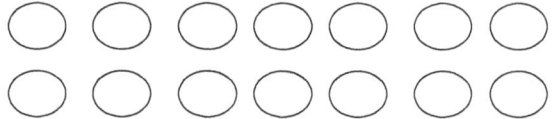

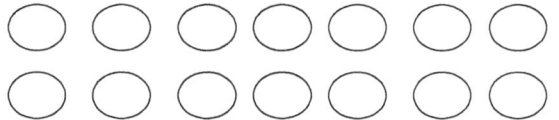

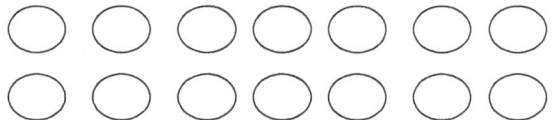

◯ ◯ ◯ ◯ ◯ ◯ ◯
◯ ◯ ◯ ◯ ◯ ◯ ◯

| WORKOUT | TIME | DURATION | CALORIES BURNED |
|---------|------|----------|-----------------|
| _____ | _____ | _____ | _____ |
| _____ | _____ | _____ | _____ |
| _____ | _____ | _____ | _____ |

WATER
(8-12 GLASSES PER DAY

◯ ◯ ◯ ◯ ◯ ◯ ◯
◯ ◯ ◯ ◯ ◯ ◯ ◯

| WORKOUT | TIME | DURATION | CALORIES BURNED |
|---------|------|----------|-----------------|
| _____ | _____ | _____ | _____ |
| _____ | _____ | _____ | _____ |
| _____ | _____ | _____ | _____ |

WATER
(8-12 GLASSES PER DAY

◯ ◯ ◯ ◯ ◯ ◯ ◯
◯ ◯ ◯ ◯ ◯ ◯ ◯

REMARKS:

# WORK IT OUT

| WORKOUT | TIME | DURATION | CALORIES BURNED |
|---------|------|----------|-----------------|
| _____ | _____ | _____ | _____ |
| _____ | _____ | _____ | _____ |
| _____ | _____ | _____ | _____ |

WATER
(8-12 GLASSES PER DAY

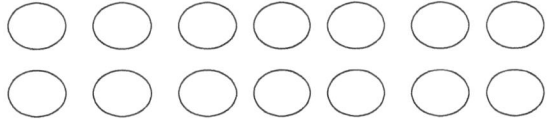

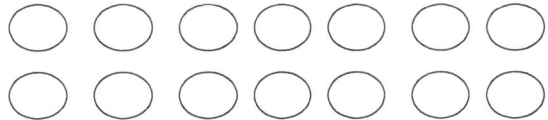

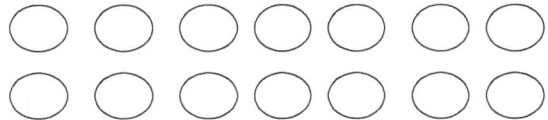

◯ ◯ ◯ ◯ ◯ ◯ ◯
◯ ◯ ◯ ◯ ◯ ◯ ◯

| WORKOUT | TIME | DURATION | CALORIES BURNED |
|---------|------|----------|-----------------|
| _____ | _____ | _____ | _____ |
| _____ | _____ | _____ | _____ |
| _____ | _____ | _____ | _____ |

WATER
(8-12 GLASSES PER DAY

◯ ◯ ◯ ◯ ◯ ◯ ◯
◯ ◯ ◯ ◯ ◯ ◯ ◯

| WORKOUT | TIME | DURATION | CALORIES BURNED |
|---------|------|----------|-----------------|
| _____ | _____ | _____ | _____ |
| _____ | _____ | _____ | _____ |
| _____ | _____ | _____ | _____ |

WATER
(8-12 GLASSES PER DAY

◯ ◯ ◯ ◯ ◯ ◯ ◯
◯ ◯ ◯ ◯ ◯ ◯ ◯

REMARKS:

# WORK IT OUT

| WORKOUT | TIME | DURATION | CALORIES BURNED |
|---------|------|----------|-----------------|
| _____ | _____ | _____ | _____ |
| _____ | _____ | _____ | _____ |
| _____ | _____ | _____ | _____ |

WATER
(8-12 GLASSES PER DAY ◯ ◯ ◯ ◯ ◯ ◯ ◯ ◯ ◯ ◯ ◯ ◯ ◯ ◯

| WORKOUT | TIME | DURATION | CALORIES BURNED |
|---------|------|----------|-----------------|
| _____ | _____ | _____ | _____ |
| _____ | _____ | _____ | _____ |
| _____ | _____ | _____ | _____ |

WATER
(8-12 GLASSES PER DAY ◯ ◯ ◯ ◯ ◯ ◯ ◯ ◯ ◯ ◯ ◯ ◯ ◯ ◯

| WORKOUT | TIME | DURATION | CALORIES BURNED |
|---------|------|----------|-----------------|
| _____ | _____ | _____ | _____ |
| _____ | _____ | _____ | _____ |
| _____ | _____ | _____ | _____ |

WATER
(8-12 GLASSES PER DAY ◯ ◯ ◯ ◯ ◯ ◯ ◯ ◯ ◯ ◯ ◯ ◯ ◯ ◯

REMARKS:

# WORK IT OUT

| WORKOUT | TIME | DURATION | CALORIES BURNED |
|---------|------|----------|-----------------|
| _____ | _____ | _____ | _____ |
| _____ | _____ | _____ | _____ |
| _____ | _____ | _____ | _____ |

WATER
(8-12 GLASSES PER DAY     ○ ○ ○ ○ ○ ○ ○
○ ○ ○ ○ ○ ○ ○

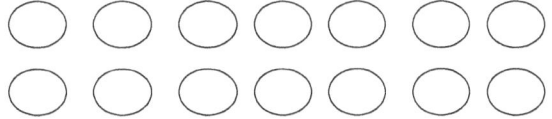

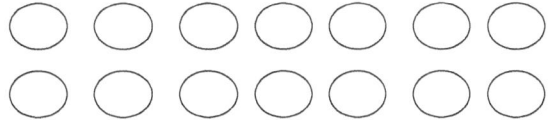

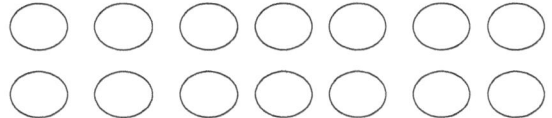

| WORKOUT | TIME | DURATION | CALORIES BURNED |
|---------|------|----------|-----------------|
| _____ | _____ | _____ | _____ |
| _____ | _____ | _____ | _____ |
| _____ | _____ | _____ | _____ |

WATER
(8-12 GLASSES PER DAY     ○ ○ ○ ○ ○ ○ ○
○ ○ ○ ○ ○ ○ ○

| WORKOUT | TIME | DURATION | CALORIES BURNED |
|---------|------|----------|-----------------|
| _____ | _____ | _____ | _____ |
| _____ | _____ | _____ | _____ |
| _____ | _____ | _____ | _____ |

WATER
(8-12 GLASSES PER DAY     ○ ○ ○ ○ ○ ○ ○
○ ○ ○ ○ ○ ○ ○

REMARKS:

# WORK IT OUT

| WORKOUT | TIME | DURATION | CALORIES BURNED |
|---------|------|----------|-----------------|
| _____ | _____ | _____ | _____ |
| _____ | _____ | _____ | _____ |
| _____ | _____ | _____ | _____ |

WATER
(8-12 GLASSES PER DAY

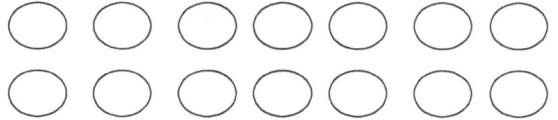

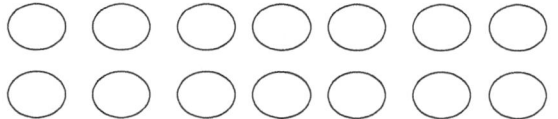

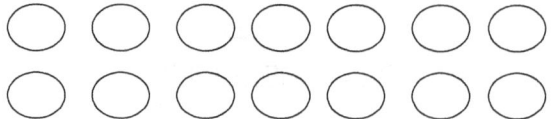

◯ ◯ ◯ ◯ ◯ ◯ ◯
◯ ◯ ◯ ◯ ◯ ◯ ◯

| WORKOUT | TIME | DURATION | CALORIES BURNED |
|---------|------|----------|-----------------|
| _____ | _____ | _____ | _____ |
| _____ | _____ | _____ | _____ |
| _____ | _____ | _____ | _____ |

WATER
(8-12 GLASSES PER DAY

◯ ◯ ◯ ◯ ◯ ◯ ◯
◯ ◯ ◯ ◯ ◯ ◯ ◯

| WORKOUT | TIME | DURATION | CALORIES BURNED |
|---------|------|----------|-----------------|
| _____ | _____ | _____ | _____ |
| _____ | _____ | _____ | _____ |
| _____ | _____ | _____ | _____ |

WATER
(8-12 GLASSES PER DAY

◯ ◯ ◯ ◯ ◯ ◯ ◯
◯ ◯ ◯ ◯ ◯ ◯ ◯

REMARKS:

# EXERCISE LOG

| DATE: | | Su M Tu W Th F Sa | |
|---|---|---|---|

| EXERCISES | SETS | TIME |
|---|---|---|
| | | |
| | | |
| | | |
| | | |
| | | |
| | | |
| | | |
| | | |
| | | |
| | | |
| | | |
| | | |
| | | |

# This Weeks

# Workout

- Record Your Weekly Workout

- Record Your Daily Workout

- Record Calories Burned

# DAILY LOG

| DATE: | | | Su M Tu W Th F Sa | |
|---|---|---|---|---|
| TIME | QTY | FOOD | CALORIES | FAT |
| | | | | |
| | | | | |
| | | | | |
| | | | | |
| | | | | |
| | | | | |
| | | | | |
| | | | | |
| | | | | |
| | | | | |
| | | | | |
| | | | | |
| | | | | |
| | | | | |
| | | | | |
| | | | | |
| | | | | |
| | | | | |
| | | | | |
| | | | | |
| | | | | |
| | | | | |
| | | | | |
| | | | | |
| | | | | |

# WORK IT OUT

| WORKOUT | TIME | DURATION | CALORIES BURNED |
|---------|------|----------|-----------------|
| _____ | _____ | _____ | _____ |
| _____ | _____ | _____ | _____ |
| _____ | _____ | _____ | _____ |

WATER
(8-12 GLASSES PER DAY     ○ ○ ○ ○ ○ ○ ○
                          ○ ○ ○ ○ ○ ○ ○

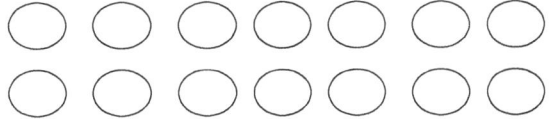

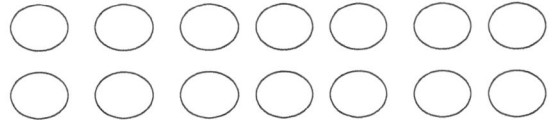

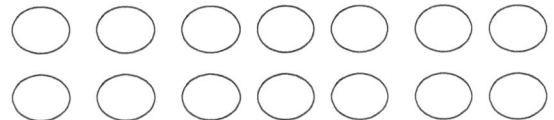

| WORKOUT | TIME | DURATION | CALORIES BURNED |
|---------|------|----------|-----------------|
| _____ | _____ | _____ | _____ |
| _____ | _____ | _____ | _____ |
| _____ | _____ | _____ | _____ |

WATER
(8-12 GLASSES PER DAY     ○ ○ ○ ○ ○ ○ ○
                          ○ ○ ○ ○ ○ ○ ○

| WORKOUT | TIME | DURATION | CALORIES BURNED |
|---------|------|----------|-----------------|
| _____ | _____ | _____ | _____ |
| _____ | _____ | _____ | _____ |

WATER
(8-12 GLASSES PER DAY     ○ ○ ○ ○ ○ ○ ○
                          ○ ○ ○ ○ ○ ○ ○

REMARKS:

# WORK IT OUT

| WORKOUT | TIME | DURATION | CALORIES BURNED |
|---------|------|----------|-----------------|
| _____ | _____ | _____ | _____ |
| _____ | _____ | _____ | _____ |
| _____ | _____ | _____ | _____ |

WATER
(8-12 GLASSES PER DAY

◯ ◯ ◯ ◯ ◯ ◯ ◯
◯ ◯ ◯ ◯ ◯ ◯ ◯

| WORKOUT | TIME | DURATION | CALORIES BURNED |
|---------|------|----------|-----------------|
| _____ | _____ | _____ | _____ |
| _____ | _____ | _____ | _____ |
| _____ | _____ | _____ | _____ |

WATER
(8-12 GLASSES PER DAY

◯ ◯ ◯ ◯ ◯ ◯ ◯
◯ ◯ ◯ ◯ ◯ ◯ ◯

| WORKOUT | TIME | DURATION | CALORIES BURNED |
|---------|------|----------|-----------------|
| _____ | _____ | _____ | _____ |
| _____ | _____ | _____ | _____ |
| _____ | _____ | _____ | _____ |

WATER
(8-12 GLASSES PER DAY

◯ ◯ ◯ ◯ ◯ ◯ ◯
◯ ◯ ◯ ◯ ◯ ◯ ◯

REMARKS:

# WORK IT OUT

| WORKOUT | TIME | DURATION | CALORIES BURNED |
|---------|------|----------|-----------------|
| _____ | _____ | _____ | _____ |
| _____ | _____ | _____ | _____ |
| _____ | _____ | _____ | _____ |

WATER
(8-12 GLASSES PER DAY

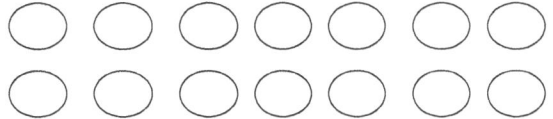

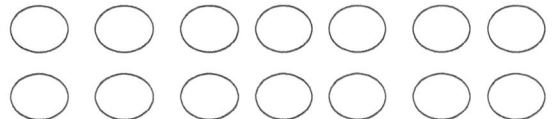

◯ ◯ ◯ ◯ ◯ ◯ ◯
◯ ◯ ◯ ◯ ◯ ◯ ◯

| WORKOUT | TIME | DURATION | CALORIES BURNED |
|---------|------|----------|-----------------|
| _____ | _____ | _____ | _____ |
| _____ | _____ | _____ | _____ |
| _____ | _____ | _____ | _____ |

WATER
(8-12 GLASSES PER DAY

◯ ◯ ◯ ◯ ◯ ◯ ◯
◯ ◯ ◯ ◯ ◯ ◯ ◯

| WORKOUT | TIME | DURATION | CALORIES BURNED |
|---------|------|----------|-----------------|
| _____ | _____ | _____ | _____ |
| _____ | _____ | _____ | _____ |
| _____ | _____ | _____ | _____ |

WATER
(8-12 GLASSES PER DAY

◯ ◯ ◯ ◯ ◯ ◯ ◯
◯ ◯ ◯ ◯ ◯ ◯ ◯

REMARKS:

# WORK IT OUT

| WORKOUT | TIME | DURATION | CALORIES BURNED |
|---------|------|----------|-----------------|
| _____ | _____ | _____ | _____ |
| _____ | _____ | _____ | _____ |
| _____ | _____ | _____ | _____ |

WATER
(8-12 GLASSES PER DAY

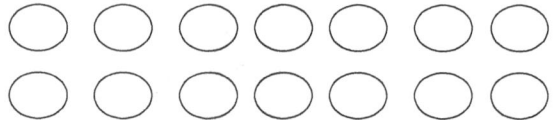

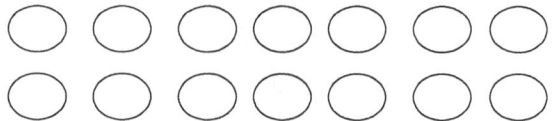

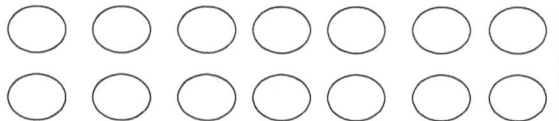

◯ ◯ ◯ ◯ ◯ ◯ ◯
◯ ◯ ◯ ◯ ◯ ◯ ◯

| WORKOUT | TIME | DURATION | CALORIES BURNED |
|---------|------|----------|-----------------|
| _____ | _____ | _____ | _____ |
| _____ | _____ | _____ | _____ |
| _____ | _____ | _____ | _____ |

WATER
(8-12 GLASSES PER DAY

◯ ◯ ◯ ◯ ◯ ◯ ◯
◯ ◯ ◯ ◯ ◯ ◯ ◯

| WORKOUT | TIME | DURATION | CALORIES BURNED |
|---------|------|----------|-----------------|
| _____ | _____ | _____ | _____ |
| _____ | _____ | _____ | _____ |
| _____ | _____ | _____ | _____ |

WATER
(8-12 GLASSES PER DAY

◯ ◯ ◯ ◯ ◯ ◯ ◯
◯ ◯ ◯ ◯ ◯ ◯ ◯

REMARKS:

# WORK IT OUT

| WORKOUT | TIME | DURATION | CALORIES BURNED |
|---------|------|----------|-----------------|
| _____ | _____ | _____ | _____ |
| _____ | _____ | _____ | _____ |
| _____ | _____ | _____ | _____ |

WATER
(8-12 GLASSES PER DAY

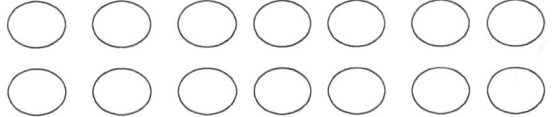

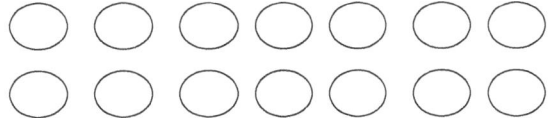

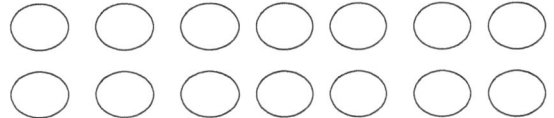

◯ ◯ ◯ ◯ ◯ ◯ ◯
◯ ◯ ◯ ◯ ◯ ◯ ◯

| WORKOUT | TIME | DURATION | CALORIES BURNED |
|---------|------|----------|-----------------|
| _____ | _____ | _____ | _____ |
| _____ | _____ | _____ | _____ |
| _____ | _____ | _____ | _____ |

WATER
(8-12 GLASSES PER DAY

◯ ◯ ◯ ◯ ◯ ◯ ◯
◯ ◯ ◯ ◯ ◯ ◯ ◯

| WORKOUT | TIME | DURATION | CALORIES BURNED |
|---------|------|----------|-----------------|
| _____ | _____ | _____ | _____ |
| _____ | _____ | _____ | _____ |
| _____ | _____ | _____ | _____ |

WATER
(8-12 GLASSES PER DAY

◯ ◯ ◯ ◯ ◯ ◯ ◯
◯ ◯ ◯ ◯ ◯ ◯ ◯

REMARKS:

# WORK IT OUT

| WORKOUT | TIME | DURATION | CALORIES BURNED |
|---------|------|----------|-----------------|
| _____ | _____ | _____ | _____ |
| _____ | _____ | _____ | _____ |
| _____ | _____ | _____ | _____ |

WATER
(8-12 GLASSES PER DAY

◯ ◯ ◯ ◯ ◯ ◯ ◯
◯ ◯ ◯ ◯ ◯ ◯ ◯

| WORKOUT | TIME | DURATION | CALORIES BURNED |
|---------|------|----------|-----------------|
| _____ | _____ | _____ | _____ |
| _____ | _____ | _____ | _____ |
| _____ | _____ | _____ | _____ |

WATER
(8-12 GLASSES PER DAY

◯ ◯ ◯ ◯ ◯ ◯ ◯
◯ ◯ ◯ ◯ ◯ ◯ ◯

| WORKOUT | TIME | DURATION | CALORIES BURNED |
|---------|------|----------|-----------------|
| _____ | _____ | _____ | _____ |
| _____ | _____ | _____ | _____ |
| _____ | _____ | _____ | _____ |

WATER
(8-12 GLASSES PER DAY

◯ ◯ ◯ ◯ ◯ ◯ ◯
◯ ◯ ◯ ◯ ◯ ◯ ◯

REMARKS:

# WORK IT OUT

| WORKOUT | TIME | DURATION | CALORIES BURNED |
|---------|------|----------|-----------------|
| _____ | _____ | _____ | _____ |
| _____ | _____ | _____ | _____ |
| _____ | _____ | _____ | _____ |

WATER
(8-12 GLASSES PER DAY

◯ ◯ ◯ ◯ ◯ ◯ ◯
◯ ◯ ◯ ◯ ◯ ◯ ◯

| WORKOUT | TIME | DURATION | CALORIES BURNED |
|---------|------|----------|-----------------|
| _____ | _____ | _____ | _____ |
| _____ | _____ | _____ | _____ |
| _____ | _____ | _____ | _____ |

WATER
(8-12 GLASSES PER DAY

◯ ◯ ◯ ◯ ◯ ◯ ◯
◯ ◯ ◯ ◯ ◯ ◯ ◯

| WORKOUT | TIME | DURATION | CALORIES BURNED |
|---------|------|----------|-----------------|
| _____ | _____ | _____ | _____ |
| _____ | _____ | _____ | _____ |
| _____ | _____ | _____ | _____ |

WATER
(8-12 GLASSES PER DAY

◯ ◯ ◯ ◯ ◯ ◯ ◯
◯ ◯ ◯ ◯ ◯ ◯ ◯

REMARKS:

# EXERCISE LOG

| DATE: | Su M Tu W Th F Sa |
|---|---|

| EXERCISES | SETS | TIME |
|---|---|---|
|  |  |  |
|  |  |  |
|  |  |  |
|  |  |  |
|  |  |  |
|  |  |  |
|  |  |  |
|  |  |  |
|  |  |  |
|  |  |  |
|  |  |  |
|  |  |  |
|  |  |  |

# This Weeks

# Workout

- Record Your Weekly Workout

- Record Your Daily Workout

- Record Calories Burned

# DAILY LOG

| DATE: | | | Su M Tu W Th F Sa | |
|-------|-----|------|----------|-----|
| TIME | QTY | FOOD | CALORIES | FAT |
| | | | | |
| | | | | |
| | | | | |
| | | | | |
| | | | | |
| | | | | |
| | | | | |
| | | | | |
| | | | | |
| | | | | |
| | | | | |
| | | | | |
| | | | | |
| | | | | |
| | | | | |
| | | | | |
| | | | | |
| | | | | |
| | | | | |
| | | | | |
| | | | | |
| | | | | |
| | | | | |
| | | | | |
| | | | | |
| | | | | |
| | | | | |

# WORK IT OUT

| WORKOUT | TIME | DURATION | CALORIES BURNED |
|---------|------|----------|-----------------|
| _____ | _____ | _____ | _____ |
| _____ | _____ | _____ | _____ |
| _____ | _____ | _____ | _____ |

WATER
(8-12 GLASSES PER DAY

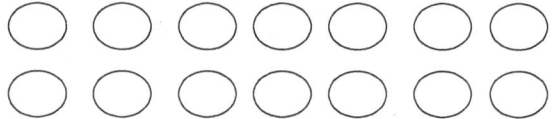

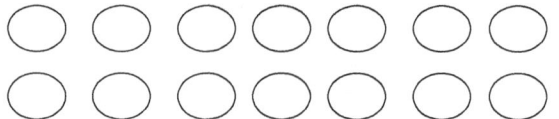

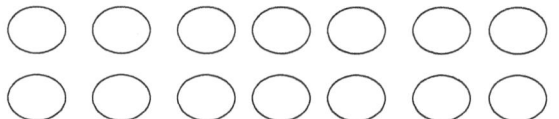

◯ ◯ ◯ ◯ ◯ ◯ ◯
◯ ◯ ◯ ◯ ◯ ◯ ◯

| WORKOUT | TIME | DURATION | CALORIES BURNED |
|---------|------|----------|-----------------|
| _____ | _____ | _____ | _____ |
| _____ | _____ | _____ | _____ |
| _____ | _____ | _____ | _____ |

WATER
(8-12 GLASSES PER DAY

◯ ◯ ◯ ◯ ◯ ◯ ◯
◯ ◯ ◯ ◯ ◯ ◯ ◯

| WORKOUT | TIME | DURATION | CALORIES BURNED |
|---------|------|----------|-----------------|
| _____ | _____ | _____ | _____ |
| _____ | _____ | _____ | _____ |
| _____ | _____ | _____ | _____ |

WATER
(8-12 GLASSES PER DAY

◯ ◯ ◯ ◯ ◯ ◯ ◯
◯ ◯ ◯ ◯ ◯ ◯ ◯

REMARKS:

# WORK IT OUT

| WORKOUT | TIME | DURATION | CALORIES BURNED |
|---------|------|----------|-----------------|
| _____ | _____ | _____ | _____ |
| _____ | _____ | _____ | _____ |
| _____ | _____ | _____ | _____ |

WATER
(8-12 GLASSES PER DAY

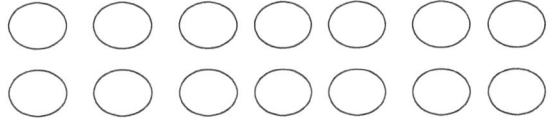

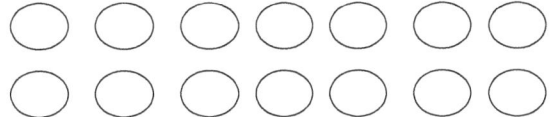

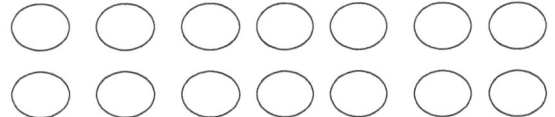

◯ ◯ ◯ ◯ ◯ ◯ ◯
◯ ◯ ◯ ◯ ◯ ◯

| WORKOUT | TIME | DURATION | CALORIES BURNED |
|---------|------|----------|-----------------|
| _____ | _____ | _____ | _____ |
| _____ | _____ | _____ | _____ |
| _____ | _____ | _____ | _____ |

WATER
(8-12 GLASSES PER DAY

◯ ◯ ◯ ◯ ◯ ◯ ◯
◯ ◯ ◯ ◯ ◯ ◯

| WORKOUT | TIME | DURATION | CALORIES BURNED |
|---------|------|----------|-----------------|
| _____ | _____ | _____ | _____ |
| _____ | _____ | _____ | _____ |
| _____ | _____ | _____ | _____ |

WATER
(8-12 GLASSES PER DAY

◯ ◯ ◯ ◯ ◯ ◯ ◯
◯ ◯ ◯ ◯ ◯ ◯

REMARKS:

# WORK IT OUT

| WORKOUT | TIME | DURATION | CALORIES BURNED |
|---------|------|----------|-----------------|
| _____ | _____ | _____ | _____ |
| _____ | _____ | _____ | _____ |
| _____ | _____ | _____ | _____ |

WATER
(8-12 GLASSES PER DAY

◯ ◯ ◯ ◯ ◯ ◯ ◯
◯ ◯ ◯ ◯ ◯ ◯ ◯

| WORKOUT | TIME | DURATION | CALORIES BURNED |
|---------|------|----------|-----------------|
| _____ | _____ | _____ | _____ |
| _____ | _____ | _____ | _____ |
| _____ | _____ | _____ | _____ |

WATER
(8-12 GLASSES PER DAY

◯ ◯ ◯ ◯ ◯ ◯ ◯
◯ ◯ ◯ ◯ ◯ ◯ ◯

| WORKOUT | TIME | DURATION | CALORIES BURNED |
|---------|------|----------|-----------------|
| _____ | _____ | _____ | _____ |
| _____ | _____ | _____ | _____ |
| _____ | _____ | _____ | _____ |

WATER
(8-12 GLASSES PER DAY

◯ ◯ ◯ ◯ ◯ ◯ ◯
◯ ◯ ◯ ◯ ◯ ◯ ◯

REMARKS:

# WORK IT OUT

| WORKOUT | TIME | DURATION | CALORIES BURNED |
|---------|------|----------|-----------------|
| _____ | _____ | _____ | _____ |
| _____ | _____ | _____ | _____ |
| _____ | _____ | _____ | _____ |

WATER
(8-12 GLASSES PER DAY

◯ ◯ ◯ ◯ ◯ ◯ ◯
◯ ◯ ◯ ◯ ◯ ◯ ◯

| WORKOUT | TIME | DURATION | CALORIES BURNED |
|---------|------|----------|-----------------|
| _____ | _____ | _____ | _____ |
| _____ | _____ | _____ | _____ |
| _____ | _____ | _____ | _____ |

WATER
(8-12 GLASSES PER DAY

◯ ◯ ◯ ◯ ◯ ◯ ◯
◯ ◯ ◯ ◯ ◯ ◯ ◯

| WORKOUT | TIME | DURATION | CALORIES BURNED |
|---------|------|----------|-----------------|
| _____ | _____ | _____ | _____ |
| _____ | _____ | _____ | _____ |
| _____ | _____ | _____ | _____ |

WATER
(8-12 GLASSES PER DAY

◯ ◯ ◯ ◯ ◯ ◯ ◯
◯ ◯ ◯ ◯ ◯ ◯ ◯

REMARKS:

# WORK IT OUT

| WORKOUT | TIME | DURATION | CALORIES BURNED |
|---------|------|----------|-----------------|
| _____ | _____ | _____ | _____ |
| _____ | _____ | _____ | _____ |
| _____ | _____ | _____ | _____ |

WATER
(8-12 GLASSES PER DAY
◯ ◯ ◯ ◯ ◯ ◯ ◯
◯ ◯ ◯ ◯ ◯ ◯ ◯

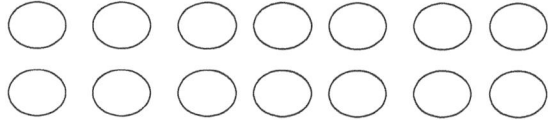

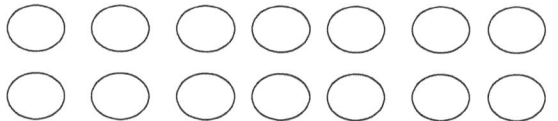

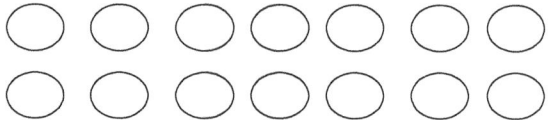

| WORKOUT | TIME | DURATION | CALORIES BURNED |
|---------|------|----------|-----------------|
| _____ | _____ | _____ | _____ |
| _____ | _____ | _____ | _____ |
| _____ | _____ | _____ | _____ |

WATER
(8-12 GLASSES PER DAY
◯ ◯ ◯ ◯ ◯ ◯ ◯
◯ ◯ ◯ ◯ ◯ ◯ ◯

| WORKOUT | TIME | DURATION | CALORIES BURNED |
|---------|------|----------|-----------------|
| _____ | _____ | _____ | _____ |
| _____ | _____ | _____ | _____ |
| _____ | _____ | _____ | _____ |

WATER
(8-12 GLASSES PER DAY
◯ ◯ ◯ ◯ ◯ ◯ ◯
◯ ◯ ◯ ◯ ◯ ◯ ◯

REMARKS:

# WORK IT OUT

| WORKOUT | TIME | DURATION | CALORIES BURNED |
|---------|------|----------|-----------------|
| _____ | _____ | _____ | _____ |
| _____ | _____ | _____ | _____ |
| _____ | _____ | _____ | _____ |

WATER
(8-12 GLASSES PER DAY

◯ ◯ ◯ ◯ ◯ ◯ ◯
◯ ◯ ◯ ◯ ◯ ◯ ◯

| WORKOUT | TIME | DURATION | CALORIES BURNED |
|---------|------|----------|-----------------|
| _____ | _____ | _____ | _____ |
| _____ | _____ | _____ | _____ |
| _____ | _____ | _____ | _____ |

WATER
(8-12 GLASSES PER DAY

◯ ◯ ◯ ◯ ◯ ◯ ◯
◯ ◯ ◯ ◯ ◯ ◯ ◯

| WORKOUT | TIME | DURATION | CALORIES BURNED |
|---------|------|----------|-----------------|
| _____ | _____ | _____ | _____ |
| _____ | _____ | _____ | _____ |
| _____ | _____ | _____ | _____ |

WATER
(8-12 GLASSES PER DAY

◯ ◯ ◯ ◯ ◯ ◯ ◯
◯ ◯ ◯ ◯ ◯ ◯ ◯

REMARKS:

# WORK IT OUT

| WORKOUT | TIME | DURATION | CALORIES BURNED |
|---------|------|----------|-----------------|
| _____ | _____ | _____ | _____ |
| _____ | _____ | _____ | _____ |
| _____ | _____ | _____ | _____ |

WATER
(8-12 GLASSES PER DAY

◯ ◯ ◯ ◯ ◯ ◯ ◯
◯ ◯ ◯ ◯ ◯ ◯ ◯

| WORKOUT | TIME | DURATION | CALORIES BURNED |
|---------|------|----------|-----------------|
| _____ | _____ | _____ | _____ |
| _____ | _____ | _____ | _____ |
| _____ | _____ | _____ | _____ |

WATER
(8-12 GLASSES PER DAY

◯ ◯ ◯ ◯ ◯ ◯ ◯
◯ ◯ ◯ ◯ ◯ ◯ ◯

| WORKOUT | TIME | DURATION | CALORIES BURNED |
|---------|------|----------|-----------------|
| _____ | _____ | _____ | _____ |
| _____ | _____ | _____ | _____ |

WATER
(8-12 GLASSES PER DAY

◯ ◯ ◯ ◯ ◯ ◯ ◯
◯ ◯ ◯ ◯ ◯ ◯ ◯

REMARKS:

# EXERCISE LOG

| DATE: | | Su M Tu W Th F Sa | |
|---|---|---|---|

| EXERCISES | SETS | TIME |
|---|---|---|
| | | |
| | | |
| | | |
| | | |
| | | |
| | | |
| | | |
| | | |
| | | |
| | | |
| | | |
| | | |
| | | |

# This Weeks

# Workout

- Record Your Weekly Workout

- Record Your Daily Workout

- Record Calories Burned

# DAILY LOG

| DATE: | | Su M Tu W Th F Sa | | |
|---|---|---|---|---|
| TIME | QTY | FOOD | CALORIES | FAT |
| | | | | |
| | | | | |
| | | | | |
| | | | | |
| | | | | |
| | | | | |
| | | | | |
| | | | | |
| | | | | |
| | | | | |
| | | | | |
| | | | | |
| | | | | |
| | | | | |
| | | | | |
| | | | | |
| | | | | |
| | | | | |
| | | | | |
| | | | | |
| | | | | |
| | | | | |
| | | | | |
| | | | | |

# WORK IT OUT

| WORKOUT | TIME | DURATION | CALORIES BURNED |
|---------|------|----------|-----------------|
| _____ | _____ | _____ | _____ |
| _____ | _____ | _____ | _____ |
| _____ | _____ | _____ | _____ |

WATER
(8-12 GLASSES PER DAY

◯ ◯ ◯ ◯ ◯ ◯ ◯
◯ ◯ ◯ ◯ ◯ ◯ ◯

| WORKOUT | TIME | DURATION | CALORIES BURNED |
|---------|------|----------|-----------------|
| _____ | _____ | _____ | _____ |
| _____ | _____ | _____ | _____ |
| _____ | _____ | _____ | _____ |

WATER
(8-12 GLASSES PER DAY

◯ ◯ ◯ ◯ ◯ ◯ ◯
◯ ◯ ◯ ◯ ◯ ◯ ◯

| WORKOUT | TIME | DURATION | CALORIES BURNED |
|---------|------|----------|-----------------|
| _____ | _____ | _____ | _____ |
| _____ | _____ | _____ | _____ |
| _____ | _____ | _____ | _____ |

WATER
(8-12 GLASSES PER DAY

◯ ◯ ◯ ◯ ◯ ◯ ◯
◯ ◯ ◯ ◯ ◯ ◯ ◯

REMARKS:

# WORK IT OUT

| WORKOUT | TIME | DURATION | CALORIES BURNED |
|---------|------|----------|-----------------|
| _____ | _____ | _____ | _____ |
| _____ | _____ | _____ | _____ |
| _____ | _____ | _____ | _____ |

WATER
(8-12 GLASSES PER DAY

◯ ◯ ◯ ◯ ◯ ◯ ◯
◯ ◯ ◯ ◯ ◯ ◯ ◯

| WORKOUT | TIME | DURATION | CALORIES BURNED |
|---------|------|----------|-----------------|
| _____ | _____ | _____ | _____ |
| _____ | _____ | _____ | _____ |
| _____ | _____ | _____ | _____ |

WATER
(8-12 GLASSES PER DAY

◯ ◯ ◯ ◯ ◯ ◯ ◯
◯ ◯ ◯ ◯ ◯ ◯ ◯

| WORKOUT | TIME | DURATION | CALORIES BURNED |
|---------|------|----------|-----------------|
| _____ | _____ | _____ | _____ |
| _____ | _____ | _____ | _____ |
| _____ | _____ | _____ | _____ |

WATER
(8-12 GLASSES PER DAY

◯ ◯ ◯ ◯ ◯ ◯ ◯
◯ ◯ ◯ ◯ ◯ ◯ ◯

REMARKS:

# WORK IT OUT

| WORKOUT | TIME | DURATION | CALORIES BURNED |
|---------|------|----------|-----------------|
| _____ | _____ | _____ | _____ |
| _____ | _____ | _____ | _____ |
| _____ | _____ | _____ | _____ |

WATER
(8-12 GLASSES PER DAY

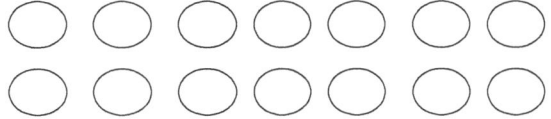

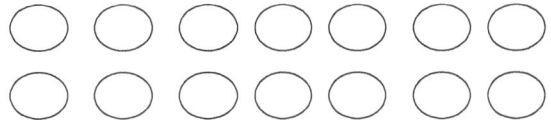

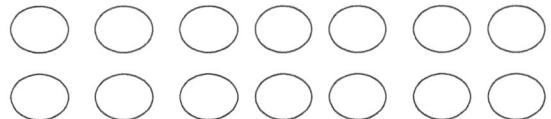

◯ ◯ ◯ ◯ ◯ ◯ ◯
◯ ◯ ◯ ◯ ◯ ◯ ◯

| WORKOUT | TIME | DURATION | CALORIES BURNED |
|---------|------|----------|-----------------|
| _____ | _____ | _____ | _____ |
| _____ | _____ | _____ | _____ |
| _____ | _____ | _____ | _____ |

WATER
(8-12 GLASSES PER DAY

◯ ◯ ◯ ◯ ◯ ◯ ◯
◯ ◯ ◯ ◯ ◯ ◯ ◯

| WORKOUT | TIME | DURATION | CALORIES BURNED |
|---------|------|----------|-----------------|
| _____ | _____ | _____ | _____ |
| _____ | _____ | _____ | _____ |
| _____ | _____ | _____ | _____ |

WATER
(8-12 GLASSES PER DAY

◯ ◯ ◯ ◯ ◯ ◯ ◯
◯ ◯ ◯ ◯ ◯ ◯ ◯

REMARKS:

# WORK IT OUT

| WORKOUT | TIME | DURATION | CALORIES BURNED |
|---------|------|----------|-----------------|
| _____ | _____ | _____ | _____ |
| _____ | _____ | _____ | _____ |
| _____ | _____ | _____ | _____ |

WATER
(8-12 GLASSES PER DAY

○ ○ ○ ○ ○ ○ ○
○ ○ ○ ○ ○ ○ ○

| WORKOUT | TIME | DURATION | CALORIES BURNED |
|---------|------|----------|-----------------|
| _____ | _____ | _____ | _____ |
| _____ | _____ | _____ | _____ |
| _____ | _____ | _____ | _____ |

WATER
(8-12 GLASSES PER DAY

○ ○ ○ ○ ○ ○ ○
○ ○ ○ ○ ○ ○ ○

| WORKOUT | TIME | DURATION | CALORIES BURNED |
|---------|------|----------|-----------------|
| _____ | _____ | _____ | _____ |
| _____ | _____ | _____ | _____ |
| _____ | _____ | _____ | _____ |

WATER
(8-12 GLASSES PER DAY

○ ○ ○ ○ ○ ○ ○
○ ○ ○ ○ ○ ○ ○

REMARKS:

# WORK IT OUT

| WORKOUT | TIME | DURATION | CALORIES BURNED |
|---------|------|----------|-----------------|
| _____ | _____ | _____ | _____ |
| _____ | _____ | _____ | _____ |
| _____ | _____ | _____ | _____ |

WATER
(8-12 GLASSES PER DAY

◯ ◯ ◯ ◯ ◯ ◯ ◯
◯ ◯ ◯ ◯ ◯ ◯ ◯

| WORKOUT | TIME | DURATION | CALORIES BURNED |
|---------|------|----------|-----------------|
| _____ | _____ | _____ | _____ |
| _____ | _____ | _____ | _____ |
| _____ | _____ | _____ | _____ |

WATER
(8-12 GLASSES PER DAY

◯ ◯ ◯ ◯ ◯ ◯ ◯
◯ ◯ ◯ ◯ ◯ ◯ ◯

| WORKOUT | TIME | DURATION | CALORIES BURNED |
|---------|------|----------|-----------------|
| _____ | _____ | _____ | _____ |
| _____ | _____ | _____ | _____ |
| _____ | _____ | _____ | _____ |

WATER
(8-12 GLASSES PER DAY

◯ ◯ ◯ ◯ ◯ ◯ ◯
◯ ◯ ◯ ◯ ◯ ◯ ◯

REMARKS:

# WORK IT OUT

| WORKOUT | TIME | DURATION | CALORIES BURNED |
|---------|------|----------|-----------------|
| _____ | _____ | _____ | _____ |
| _____ | _____ | _____ | _____ |
| _____ | _____ | _____ | _____ |

WATER
(8-12 GLASSES PER DAY

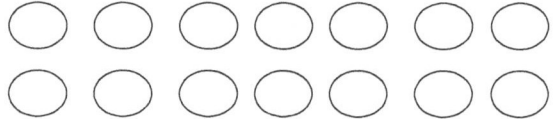

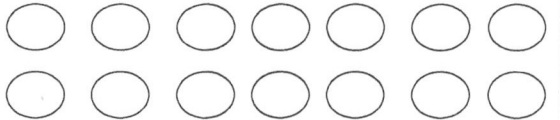

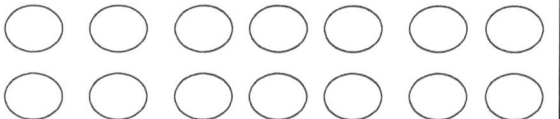

◯ ◯ ◯ ◯ ◯ ◯ ◯
◯ ◯ ◯ ◯ ◯ ◯ ◯

| WORKOUT | TIME | DURATION | CALORIES BURNED |
|---------|------|----------|-----------------|
| _____ | _____ | _____ | _____ |
| _____ | _____ | _____ | _____ |
| _____ | _____ | _____ | _____ |

WATER
(8-12 GLASSES PER DAY

◯ ◯ ◯ ◯ ◯ ◯ ◯
◯ ◯ ◯ ◯ ◯ ◯ ◯

| WORKOUT | TIME | DURATION | CALORIES BURNED |
|---------|------|----------|-----------------|
| _____ | _____ | _____ | _____ |
| _____ | _____ | _____ | _____ |
| _____ | _____ | _____ | _____ |

WATER
(8-12 GLASSES PER DAY

◯ ◯ ◯ ◯ ◯ ◯ ◯
◯ ◯ ◯ ◯ ◯ ◯ ◯

REMARKS:

# WORK IT OUT

| WORKOUT | TIME | DURATION | CALORIES BURNED |
|---------|------|----------|-----------------|
| _____ | _____ | _____ | _____ |
| _____ | _____ | _____ | _____ |
| _____ | _____ | _____ | _____ |

WATER
(8-12 GLASSES PER DAY

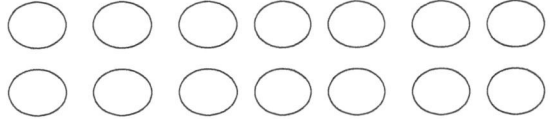

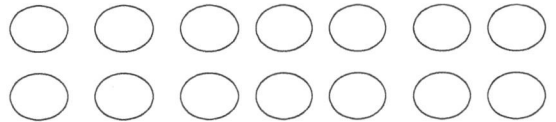

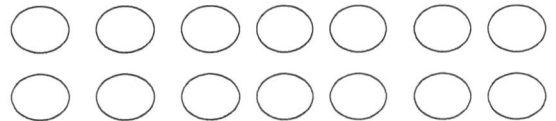

○ ○ ○ ○ ○ ○ ○
○ ○ ○ ○ ○ ○

| WORKOUT | TIME | DURATION | CALORIES BURNED |
|---------|------|----------|-----------------|
| _____ | _____ | _____ | _____ |
| _____ | _____ | _____ | _____ |
| _____ | _____ | _____ | _____ |

WATER
(8-12 GLASSES PER DAY

○ ○ ○ ○ ○ ○ ○
○ ○ ○ ○ ○ ○

| WORKOUT | TIME | DURATION | CALORIES BURNED |
|---------|------|----------|-----------------|
| _____ | _____ | _____ | _____ |
| _____ | _____ | _____ | _____ |
| _____ | _____ | _____ | _____ |

WATER
(8-12 GLASSES PER DAY

○ ○ ○ ○ ○ ○ ○
○ ○ ○ ○ ○ ○

REMARKS:

# EXERCISE LOG

| DATE: | Su M Tu W Th F Sa |
|-------|-------------------|

| EXERCISES | SETS | TIME |
|-----------|------|------|
|  |  |  |
|  |  |  |
|  |  |  |
|  |  |  |
|  |  |  |
|  |  |  |
|  |  |  |
|  |  |  |
|  |  |  |
|  |  |  |
|  |  |  |
|  |  |  |
|  |  |  |

# This Weeks

# Workout

- Record Your Weekly Workout

- Record Your Daily Workout

- Record Calories Burned

# DAILY LOG

| DATE: | | | Su M Tu W Th F Sa | |
|---|---|---|---|---|
| TIME | QTY | FOOD | CALORIES | FAT |
| | | | | |
| | | | | |
| | | | | |
| | | | | |
| | | | | |
| | | | | |
| | | | | |
| | | | | |
| | | | | |
| | | | | |
| | | | | |
| | | | | |
| | | | | |
| | | | | |
| | | | | |
| | | | | |
| | | | | |
| | | | | |
| | | | | |
| | | | | |
| | | | | |
| | | | | |
| | | | | |
| | | | | |
| | | | | |

# WORK IT OUT

| WORKOUT | TIME | DURATION | CALORIES BURNED |
|---------|------|----------|-----------------|
| _____ | _____ | _____ | _____ |
| _____ | _____ | _____ | _____ |
| _____ | _____ | _____ | _____ |

WATER
(8-12 GLASSES PER DAY

◯ ◯ ◯ ◯ ◯ ◯ ◯
◯ ◯ ◯ ◯ ◯ ◯ ◯

| WORKOUT | TIME | DURATION | CALORIES BURNED |
|---------|------|----------|-----------------|
| _____ | _____ | _____ | _____ |
| _____ | _____ | _____ | _____ |
| _____ | _____ | _____ | _____ |

WATER
(8-12 GLASSES PER DAY

◯ ◯ ◯ ◯ ◯ ◯ ◯
◯ ◯ ◯ ◯ ◯ ◯ ◯

| WORKOUT | TIME | DURATION | CALORIES BURNED |
|---------|------|----------|-----------------|
| _____ | _____ | _____ | _____ |
| _____ | _____ | _____ | _____ |
| _____ | _____ | _____ | _____ |

WATER
(8-12 GLASSES PER DAY

◯ ◯ ◯ ◯ ◯ ◯ ◯
◯ ◯ ◯ ◯ ◯ ◯ ◯

REMARKS:

# WORK IT OUT

| WORKOUT | TIME | DURATION | CALORIES BURNED |
|---------|------|----------|-----------------|
| _____ | _____ | _____ | _____ |
| _____ | _____ | _____ | _____ |
| _____ | _____ | _____ | _____ |

WATER
(8-12 GLASSES PER DAY

◯ ◯ ◯ ◯ ◯ ◯ ◯
◯ ◯ ◯ ◯ ◯ ◯ ◯

| WORKOUT | TIME | DURATION | CALORIES BURNED |
|---------|------|----------|-----------------|
| _____ | _____ | _____ | _____ |
| _____ | _____ | _____ | _____ |
| _____ | _____ | _____ | _____ |

WATER
(8-12 GLASSES PER DAY

◯ ◯ ◯ ◯ ◯ ◯ ◯
◯ ◯ ◯ ◯ ◯ ◯ ◯

| WORKOUT | TIME | DURATION | CALORIES BURNED |
|---------|------|----------|-----------------|
| _____ | _____ | _____ | _____ |
| _____ | _____ | _____ | _____ |
| _____ | _____ | _____ | _____ |

WATER
(8-12 GLASSES PER DAY

◯ ◯ ◯ ◯ ◯ ◯ ◯
◯ ◯ ◯ ◯ ◯ ◯ ◯

REMARKS:

# WORK IT OUT

| WORKOUT | TIME | DURATION | CALORIES BURNED |
|---------|------|----------|-----------------|
| _____ | _____ | _____ | _____ |
| _____ | _____ | _____ | _____ |
| _____ | _____ | _____ | _____ |

WATER
(8-12 GLASSES PER DAY

◯ ◯ ◯ ◯ ◯ ◯ ◯
◯ ◯ ◯ ◯ ◯ ◯ ◯

| WORKOUT | TIME | DURATION | CALORIES BURNED |
|---------|------|----------|-----------------|
| _____ | _____ | _____ | _____ |
| _____ | _____ | _____ | _____ |
| _____ | _____ | _____ | _____ |

WATER
(8-12 GLASSES PER DAY

◯ ◯ ◯ ◯ ◯ ◯ ◯
◯ ◯ ◯ ◯ ◯ ◯ ◯

| WORKOUT | TIME | DURATION | CALORIES BURNED |
|---------|------|----------|-----------------|
| _____ | _____ | _____ | _____ |
| _____ | _____ | _____ | _____ |
| _____ | _____ | _____ | _____ |

WATER
(8-12 GLASSES PER DAY

◯ ◯ ◯ ◯ ◯ ◯ ◯
◯ ◯ ◯ ◯ ◯ ◯ ◯

REMARKS:

# WORK IT OUT

| WORKOUT | TIME | DURATION | CALORIES BURNED |
|---------|------|----------|-----------------|
| _____ | _____ | _____ | _____ |
| _____ | _____ | _____ | _____ |
| _____ | _____ | _____ | _____ |

WATER
(8-12 GLASSES PER DAY

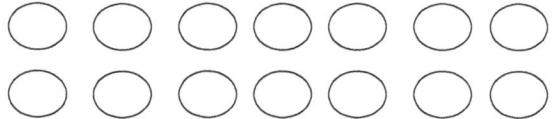

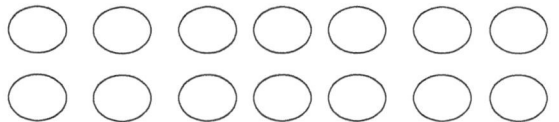

◯ ◯ ◯ ◯ ◯ ◯ ◯
◯ ◯ ◯ ◯ ◯ ◯ ◯

| WORKOUT | TIME | DURATION | CALORIES BURNED |
|---------|------|----------|-----------------|
| _____ | _____ | _____ | _____ |
| _____ | _____ | _____ | _____ |
| _____ | _____ | _____ | _____ |

WATER
(8-12 GLASSES PER DAY

◯ ◯ ◯ ◯ ◯ ◯ ◯
◯ ◯ ◯ ◯ ◯ ◯ ◯

| WORKOUT | TIME | DURATION | CALORIES BURNED |
|---------|------|----------|-----------------|
| _____ | _____ | _____ | _____ |
| _____ | _____ | _____ | _____ |
| _____ | _____ | _____ | _____ |

WATER
(8-12 GLASSES PER DAY

◯ ◯ ◯ ◯ ◯ ◯ ◯
◯ ◯ ◯ ◯ ◯ ◯ ◯

REMARKS:

# WORK IT OUT

| WORKOUT | TIME | DURATION | CALORIES BURNED |
|---------|------|----------|-----------------|
| _____ | _____ | _____ | _____ |
| _____ | _____ | _____ | _____ |
| _____ | _____ | _____ | _____ |

WATER
(8-12 GLASSES PER DAY

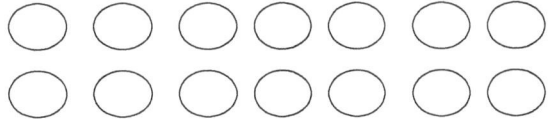

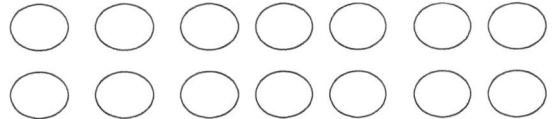

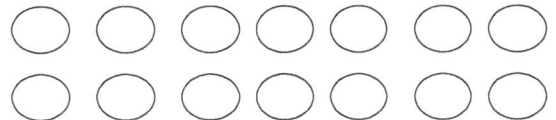

◯ ◯ ◯ ◯ ◯ ◯ ◯
◯ ◯ ◯ ◯ ◯ ◯ ◯

| WORKOUT | TIME | DURATION | CALORIES BURNED |
|---------|------|----------|-----------------|
| _____ | _____ | _____ | _____ |
| _____ | _____ | _____ | _____ |
| _____ | _____ | _____ | _____ |

WATER
(8-12 GLASSES PER DAY

◯ ◯ ◯ ◯ ◯ ◯ ◯
◯ ◯ ◯ ◯ ◯ ◯ ◯

| WORKOUT | TIME | DURATION | CALORIES BURNED |
|---------|------|----------|-----------------|
| _____ | _____ | _____ | _____ |
| _____ | _____ | _____ | _____ |
| _____ | _____ | _____ | _____ |

WATER
(8-12 GLASSES PER DAY

◯ ◯ ◯ ◯ ◯ ◯ ◯
◯ ◯ ◯ ◯ ◯ ◯ ◯

REMARKS:

# WORK IT OUT

| WORKOUT | TIME | DURATION | CALORIES BURNED |
|---------|------|----------|-----------------|
| _____ | _____ | _____ | _____ |
| _____ | _____ | _____ | _____ |
| _____ | _____ | _____ | _____ |

WATER
(8-12 GLASSES PER DAY

◯ ◯ ◯ ◯ ◯ ◯ ◯
◯ ◯ ◯ ◯ ◯ ◯

| WORKOUT | TIME | DURATION | CALORIES BURNED |
|---------|------|----------|-----------------|
| _____ | _____ | _____ | _____ |
| _____ | _____ | _____ | _____ |
| _____ | _____ | _____ | _____ |

WATER
(8-12 GLASSES PER DAY

◯ ◯ ◯ ◯ ◯ ◯ ◯
◯ ◯ ◯ ◯ ◯ ◯

| WORKOUT | TIME | DURATION | CALORIES BURNED |
|---------|------|----------|-----------------|
| _____ | _____ | _____ | _____ |
| _____ | _____ | _____ | _____ |
| _____ | _____ | _____ | _____ |

WATER
(8-12 GLASSES PER DAY

◯ ◯ ◯ ◯ ◯ ◯ ◯
◯ ◯ ◯ ◯ ◯ ◯

REMARKS:

# WORK IT OUT

| WORKOUT | TIME | DURATION | CALORIES BURNED |
|---------|------|----------|-----------------|
| _____ | _____ | _____ | _____ |
| _____ | _____ | _____ | _____ |
| _____ | _____ | _____ | _____ |

WATER
(8-12 GLASSES PER DAY

◯ ◯ ◯ ◯ ◯ ◯ ◯
◯ ◯ ◯ ◯ ◯ ◯ ◯

| WORKOUT | TIME | DURATION | CALORIES BURNED |
|---------|------|----------|-----------------|
| _____ | _____ | _____ | _____ |
| _____ | _____ | _____ | _____ |
| _____ | _____ | _____ | _____ |

WATER
(8-12 GLASSES PER DAY

◯ ◯ ◯ ◯ ◯ ◯ ◯
◯ ◯ ◯ ◯ ◯ ◯ ◯

| WORKOUT | TIME | DURATION | CALORIES BURNED |
|---------|------|----------|-----------------|
| _____ | _____ | _____ | _____ |
| _____ | _____ | _____ | _____ |
| _____ | _____ | _____ | _____ |

WATER
(8-12 GLASSES PER DAY

◯ ◯ ◯ ◯ ◯ ◯ ◯
◯ ◯ ◯ ◯ ◯ ◯ ◯

REMARKS:

# EXERCISE LOG

| DATE: | Su M Tu W Th F Sa |
|---|---|

| EXERCISES | SETS | TIME |
|---|---|---|
| | | |
| | | |
| | | |
| | | |
| | | |
| | | |
| | | |
| | | |
| | | |
| | | |
| | | |
| | | |
| | | |

# This Weeks

# Workout

- Record Your Weekly Workout

- Record Your Daily Workout

- Record Calories Burned

# DAILY LOG

| DATE: | | | Su M Tu W Th F Sa | |
|---|---|---|---|---|
| TIME | QTY | FOOD | CALORIES | FAT |
| | | | | |
| | | | | |
| | | | | |
| | | | | |
| | | | | |
| | | | | |
| | | | | |
| | | | | |
| | | | | |
| | | | | |
| | | | | |
| | | | | |
| | | | | |
| | | | | |
| | | | | |
| | | | | |
| | | | | |
| | | | | |
| | | | | |
| | | | | |
| | | | | |
| | | | | |
| | | | | |

# WORK IT OUT

| WORKOUT | TIME | DURATION | CALORIES BURNED |
|---------|------|----------|-----------------|
| _____ | _____ | _____ | _____ |
| _____ | _____ | _____ | _____ |
| _____ | _____ | _____ | _____ |

WATER
(8-12 GLASSES PER DAY

◯ ◯ ◯ ◯ ◯ ◯ ◯
◯ ◯ ◯ ◯ ◯ ◯ ◯

| WORKOUT | TIME | DURATION | CALORIES BURNED |
|---------|------|----------|-----------------|
| _____ | _____ | _____ | _____ |
| _____ | _____ | _____ | _____ |
| _____ | _____ | _____ | _____ |

WATER
(8-12 GLASSES PER DAY

◯ ◯ ◯ ◯ ◯ ◯ ◯
◯ ◯ ◯ ◯ ◯ ◯ ◯

| WORKOUT | TIME | DURATION | CALORIES BURNED |
|---------|------|----------|-----------------|
| _____ | _____ | _____ | _____ |
| _____ | _____ | _____ | _____ |
| _____ | _____ | _____ | _____ |

WATER
(8-12 GLASSES PER DAY

◯ ◯ ◯ ◯ ◯ ◯ ◯
◯ ◯ ◯ ◯ ◯ ◯ ◯

REMARKS:

# WORK IT OUT

| WORKOUT | TIME | DURATION | CALORIES BURNED |
|---------|------|----------|-----------------|
| _____ | _____ | _____ | _____ |
| _____ | _____ | _____ | _____ |
| _____ | _____ | _____ | _____ |

WATER
(8-12 GLASSES PER DAY

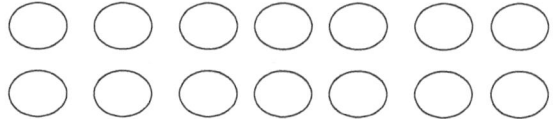

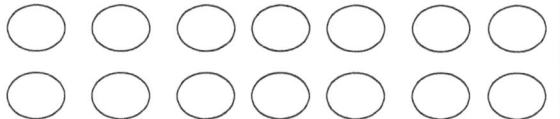

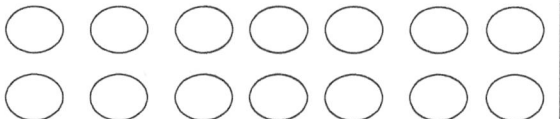

◯ ◯ ◯ ◯ ◯ ◯ ◯
◯ ◯ ◯ ◯ ◯ ◯ ◯

| WORKOUT | TIME | DURATION | CALORIES BURNED |
|---------|------|----------|-----------------|
| _____ | _____ | _____ | _____ |
| _____ | _____ | _____ | _____ |
| _____ | _____ | _____ | _____ |

WATER
(8-12 GLASSES PER DAY

◯ ◯ ◯ ◯ ◯ ◯ ◯
◯ ◯ ◯ ◯ ◯ ◯ ◯

| WORKOUT | TIME | DURATION | CALORIES BURNED |
|---------|------|----------|-----------------|
| _____ | _____ | _____ | _____ |
| _____ | _____ | _____ | _____ |
| _____ | _____ | _____ | _____ |

WATER
(8-12 GLASSES PER DAY

◯ ◯ ◯ ◯ ◯ ◯ ◯
◯ ◯ ◯ ◯ ◯ ◯ ◯

REMARKS:

# WORK IT OUT

| WORKOUT | TIME | DURATION | CALORIES BURNED |
|---------|------|----------|-----------------|
| _____ | _____ | _____ | _____ |
| _____ | _____ | _____ | _____ |
| _____ | _____ | _____ | _____ |

WATER
(8-12 GLASSES PER DAY

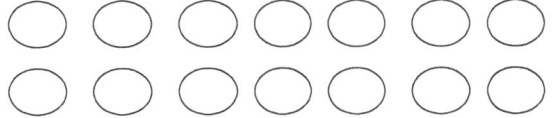

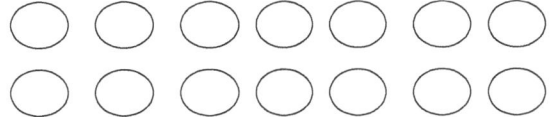

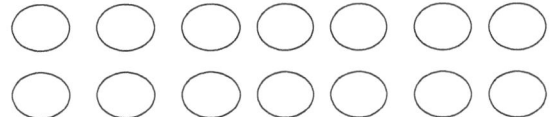

◯ ◯ ◯ ◯ ◯ ◯ ◯
◯ ◯ ◯ ◯ ◯ ◯ ◯

| WORKOUT | TIME | DURATION | CALORIES BURNED |
|---------|------|----------|-----------------|
| _____ | _____ | _____ | _____ |
| _____ | _____ | _____ | _____ |
| _____ | _____ | _____ | _____ |

WATER
(8-12 GLASSES PER DAY

◯ ◯ ◯ ◯ ◯ ◯ ◯
◯ ◯ ◯ ◯ ◯ ◯ ◯

| WORKOUT | TIME | DURATION | CALORIES BURNED |
|---------|------|----------|-----------------|
| _____ | _____ | _____ | _____ |
| _____ | _____ | _____ | _____ |
| _____ | _____ | _____ | _____ |

WATER
(8-12 GLASSES PER DAY

◯ ◯ ◯ ◯ ◯ ◯ ◯
◯ ◯ ◯ ◯ ◯ ◯ ◯

REMARKS:

# WORK IT OUT

| WORKOUT | TIME | DURATION | CALORIES BURNED |
|---------|------|----------|-----------------|
| _____ | _____ | _____ | _____ |
| _____ | _____ | _____ | _____ |
| _____ | _____ | _____ | _____ |

WATER
(8-12 GLASSES PER DAY

◯ ◯ ◯ ◯ ◯ ◯ ◯
◯ ◯ ◯ ◯ ◯ ◯ ◯

| WORKOUT | TIME | DURATION | CALORIES BURNED |
|---------|------|----------|-----------------|
| _____ | _____ | _____ | _____ |
| _____ | _____ | _____ | _____ |
| _____ | _____ | _____ | _____ |

WATER
(8-12 GLASSES PER DAY

◯ ◯ ◯ ◯ ◯ ◯ ◯
◯ ◯ ◯ ◯ ◯ ◯ ◯

| WORKOUT | TIME | DURATION | CALORIES BURNED |
|---------|------|----------|-----------------|
| _____ | _____ | _____ | _____ |
| _____ | _____ | _____ | _____ |
| _____ | _____ | _____ | _____ |

WATER
(8-12 GLASSES PER DAY

◯ ◯ ◯ ◯ ◯ ◯ ◯
◯ ◯ ◯ ◯ ◯ ◯ ◯

REMARKS:

# WORK IT OUT

| WORKOUT | TIME | DURATION | CALORIES BURNED |
|---------|------|----------|-----------------|
| _____ | _____ | _____ | _____ |
| _____ | _____ | _____ | _____ |
| _____ | _____ | _____ | _____ |

WATER
(8-12 GLASSES PER DAY

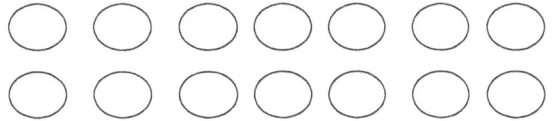

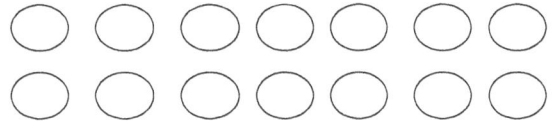

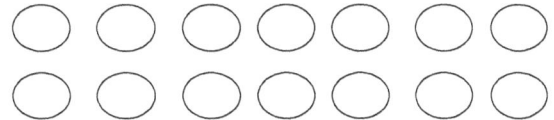

○ ○ ○ ○ ○ ○ ○
○ ○ ○ ○ ○ ○ ○

| WORKOUT | TIME | DURATION | CALORIES BURNED |
|---------|------|----------|-----------------|
| _____ | _____ | _____ | _____ |
| _____ | _____ | _____ | _____ |
| _____ | _____ | _____ | _____ |

WATER
(8-12 GLASSES PER DAY

○ ○ ○ ○ ○ ○ ○
○ ○ ○ ○ ○ ○ ○

| WORKOUT | TIME | DURATION | CALORIES BURNED |
|---------|------|----------|-----------------|
| _____ | _____ | _____ | _____ |
| _____ | _____ | _____ | _____ |
| _____ | _____ | _____ | _____ |

WATER
(8-12 GLASSES PER DAY

○ ○ ○ ○ ○ ○ ○
○ ○ ○ ○ ○ ○ ○

REMARKS:

# WORK IT OUT

| WORKOUT | TIME | DURATION | CALORIES BURNED |
|---------|------|----------|-----------------|
| _____ | _____ | _____ | _____ |
| _____ | _____ | _____ | _____ |
| _____ | _____ | _____ | _____ |

WATER
(8-12 GLASSES PER DAY

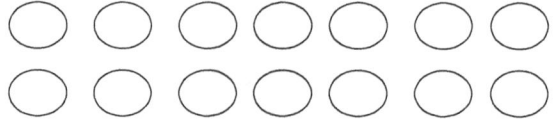

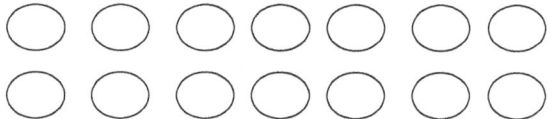

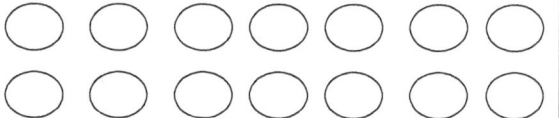

○ ○ ○ ○ ○ ○ ○
○ ○ ○ ○ ○ ○ ○

| WORKOUT | TIME | DURATION | CALORIES BURNED |
|---------|------|----------|-----------------|
| _____ | _____ | _____ | _____ |
| _____ | _____ | _____ | _____ |
| _____ | _____ | _____ | _____ |

WATER
(8-12 GLASSES PER DAY

○ ○ ○ ○ ○ ○ ○
○ ○ ○ ○ ○ ○ ○

| WORKOUT | TIME | DURATION | CALORIES BURNED |
|---------|------|----------|-----------------|
| _____ | _____ | _____ | _____ |
| _____ | _____ | _____ | _____ |
| _____ | _____ | _____ | _____ |

WATER
(8-12 GLASSES PER DAY

○ ○ ○ ○ ○ ○ ○
○ ○ ○ ○ ○ ○ ○

REMARKS:

# WORK IT OUT

| WORKOUT | TIME | DURATION | CALORIES BURNED |
|---------|------|----------|-----------------|
| _____ | _____ | _____ | _____ |
| _____ | _____ | _____ | _____ |
| _____ | _____ | _____ | _____ |

WATER
(8-12 GLASSES PER DAY

◯ ◯ ◯ ◯ ◯ ◯ ◯
◯ ◯ ◯ ◯ ◯ ◯ ◯

| WORKOUT | TIME | DURATION | CALORIES BURNED |
|---------|------|----------|-----------------|
| _____ | _____ | _____ | _____ |
| _____ | _____ | _____ | _____ |
| _____ | _____ | _____ | _____ |

WATER
(8-12 GLASSES PER DAY

◯ ◯ ◯ ◯ ◯ ◯ ◯
◯ ◯ ◯ ◯ ◯ ◯ ◯

| WORKOUT | TIME | DURATION | CALORIES BURNED |
|---------|------|----------|-----------------|
| _____ | _____ | _____ | _____ |
| _____ | _____ | _____ | _____ |
| _____ | _____ | _____ | _____ |

WATER
(8-12 GLASSES PER DAY

◯ ◯ ◯ ◯ ◯ ◯ ◯
◯ ◯ ◯ ◯ ◯ ◯ ◯

REMARKS:

# EXERCISE LOG

| DATE: | Su M Tu W Th F Sa |
| --- | --- |

| EXERCISES | SETS | TIME |
| --- | --- | --- |
|  |  |  |
|  |  |  |
|  |  |  |
|  |  |  |
|  |  |  |
|  |  |  |
|  |  |  |
|  |  |  |
|  |  |  |
|  |  |  |
|  |  |  |
|  |  |  |
|  |  |  |

# This Weeks

# Workout

- Record Your Weekly Workout

- Record Your Daily Workout

- Record Calories Burned

# DAILY LOG

| DATE: | | | Su M Tu W Th F Sa | |
|-------|-----|------|----------|-----|
| TIME | QTY | FOOD | CALORIES | FAT |
| | | | | |
| | | | | |
| | | | | |
| | | | | |
| | | | | |
| | | | | |
| | | | | |
| | | | | |
| | | | | |
| | | | | |
| | | | | |
| | | | | |
| | | | | |
| | | | | |
| | | | | |
| | | | | |
| | | | | |
| | | | | |
| | | | | |
| | | | | |
| | | | | |
| | | | | |
| | | | | |
| | | | | |

# WORK IT OUT

| WORKOUT | TIME | DURATION | CALORIES BURNED |
|---------|------|----------|-----------------|
| _____ | _____ | _____ | _____ |
| _____ | _____ | _____ | _____ |
| _____ | _____ | _____ | _____ |

WATER
(8-12 GLASSES PER DAY

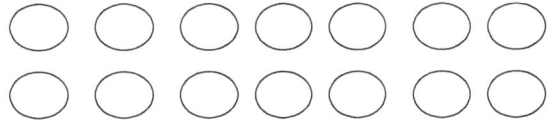

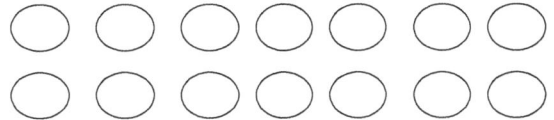

◯ ◯ ◯ ◯ ◯ ◯ ◯
◯ ◯ ◯ ◯ ◯ ◯ ◯

| WORKOUT | TIME | DURATION | CALORIES BURNED |
|---------|------|----------|-----------------|
| _____ | _____ | _____ | _____ |
| _____ | _____ | _____ | _____ |
| _____ | _____ | _____ | _____ |

WATER
(8-12 GLASSES PER DAY

◯ ◯ ◯ ◯ ◯ ◯ ◯
◯ ◯ ◯ ◯ ◯ ◯ ◯

| WORKOUT | TIME | DURATION | CALORIES BURNED |
|---------|------|----------|-----------------|
| _____ | _____ | _____ | _____ |
| _____ | _____ | _____ | _____ |
| _____ | _____ | _____ | _____ |

WATER
(8-12 GLASSES PER DAY

◯ ◯ ◯ ◯ ◯ ◯ ◯
◯ ◯ ◯ ◯ ◯ ◯ ◯

REMARKS:

# WORK IT OUT

| WORKOUT | TIME | DURATION | CALORIES BURNED |
|---------|------|----------|-----------------|
| _____ | _____ | _____ | _____ |
| _____ | _____ | _____ | _____ |
| _____ | _____ | _____ | _____ |

WATER
(8-12 GLASSES PER DAY

◯ ◯ ◯ ◯ ◯ ◯ ◯
◯ ◯ ◯ ◯ ◯ ◯ ◯

| WORKOUT | TIME | DURATION | CALORIES BURNED |
|---------|------|----------|-----------------|
| _____ | _____ | _____ | _____ |
| _____ | _____ | _____ | _____ |
| _____ | _____ | _____ | _____ |

WATER
(8-12 GLASSES PER DAY

◯ ◯ ◯ ◯ ◯ ◯ ◯
◯ ◯ ◯ ◯ ◯ ◯ ◯

| WORKOUT | TIME | DURATION | CALORIES BURNED |
|---------|------|----------|-----------------|
| _____ | _____ | _____ | _____ |
| _____ | _____ | _____ | _____ |
| _____ | _____ | _____ | _____ |

WATER
(8-12 GLASSES PER DAY

◯ ◯ ◯ ◯ ◯ ◯ ◯
◯ ◯ ◯ ◯ ◯ ◯ ◯

REMARKS:

# WORK IT OUT

| WORKOUT | TIME | DURATION | CALORIES BURNED |
|---------|------|----------|-----------------|
| _____ | _____ | _____ | _____ |
| _____ | _____ | _____ | _____ |
| _____ | _____ | _____ | _____ |

WATER
(8-12 GLASSES PER DAY   ◯ ◯ ◯ ◯ ◯ ◯ ◯
                         ◯ ◯ ◯ ◯ ◯ ◯ ◯

| WORKOUT | TIME | DURATION | CALORIES BURNED |
|---------|------|----------|-----------------|
| _____ | _____ | _____ | _____ |
| _____ | _____ | _____ | _____ |
| _____ | _____ | _____ | _____ |

WATER
(8-12 GLASSES PER DAY   ◯ ◯ ◯ ◯ ◯ ◯ ◯
                         ◯ ◯ ◯ ◯ ◯ ◯ ◯

| WORKOUT | TIME | DURATION | CALORIES BURNED |
|---------|------|----------|-----------------|
| _____ | _____ | _____ | _____ |
| _____ | _____ | _____ | _____ |
| _____ | _____ | _____ | _____ |

WATER
(8-12 GLASSES PER DAY   ◯ ◯ ◯ ◯ ◯ ◯ ◯
                         ◯ ◯ ◯ ◯ ◯ ◯ ◯

REMARKS:

# WORK IT OUT

| WORKOUT | TIME | DURATION | CALORIES BURNED |
|---|---|---|---|
| _____ | _____ | _____ | _____ |
| _____ | _____ | _____ | _____ |
| _____ | _____ | _____ | _____ |

WATER
(8-12 GLASSES PER DAY

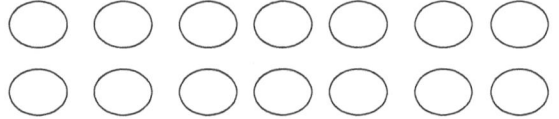

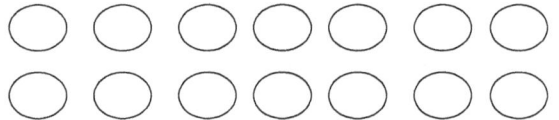

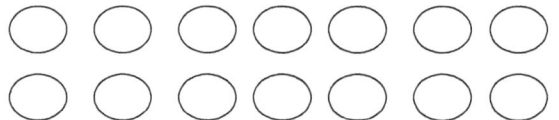

◯ ◯ ◯ ◯ ◯ ◯ ◯
◯ ◯ ◯ ◯ ◯ ◯ ◯

| WORKOUT | TIME | DURATION | CALORIES BURNED |
|---|---|---|---|
| _____ | _____ | _____ | _____ |
| _____ | _____ | _____ | _____ |
| _____ | _____ | _____ | _____ |

WATER
(8-12 GLASSES PER DAY

◯ ◯ ◯ ◯ ◯ ◯ ◯
◯ ◯ ◯ ◯ ◯ ◯ ◯

| WORKOUT | TIME | DURATION | CALORIES BURNED |
|---|---|---|---|
| _____ | _____ | _____ | _____ |
| _____ | _____ | _____ | _____ |
| _____ | _____ | _____ | _____ |

WATER
(8-12 GLASSES PER DAY

◯ ◯ ◯ ◯ ◯ ◯ ◯
◯ ◯ ◯ ◯ ◯ ◯ ◯

REMARKS:

# WORK IT OUT

| WORKOUT | TIME | DURATION | CALORIES BURNED |
|---------|------|----------|-----------------|
| _____ | _____ | _____ | _____ |
| _____ | _____ | _____ | _____ |
| _____ | _____ | _____ | _____ |

WATER
(8-12 GLASSES PER DAY

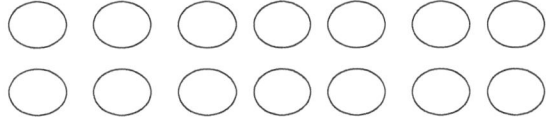

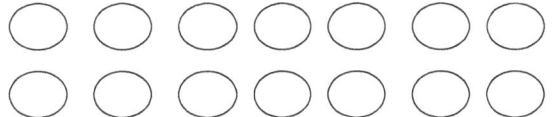

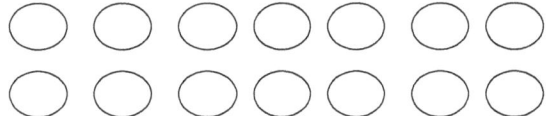

◯ ◯ ◯ ◯ ◯ ◯ ◯
◯ ◯ ◯ ◯ ◯ ◯ ◯

| WORKOUT | TIME | DURATION | CALORIES BURNED |
|---------|------|----------|-----------------|
| _____ | _____ | _____ | _____ |
| _____ | _____ | _____ | _____ |
| _____ | _____ | _____ | _____ |

WATER
(8-12 GLASSES PER DAY

◯ ◯ ◯ ◯ ◯ ◯ ◯
◯ ◯ ◯ ◯ ◯ ◯ ◯

| WORKOUT | TIME | DURATION | CALORIES BURNED |
|---------|------|----------|-----------------|
| _____ | _____ | _____ | _____ |
| _____ | _____ | _____ | _____ |
| _____ | _____ | _____ | _____ |

WATER
(8-12 GLASSES PER DAY

◯ ◯ ◯ ◯ ◯ ◯ ◯
◯ ◯ ◯ ◯ ◯ ◯ ◯

REMARKS:

# WORK IT OUT

| WORKOUT | TIME | DURATION | CALORIES BURNED |
|---------|------|----------|-----------------|
| _____ | _____ | _____ | _____ |
| _____ | _____ | _____ | _____ |
| _____ | _____ | _____ | _____ |

WATER
(8-12 GLASSES PER DAY
◯ ◯ ◯ ◯ ◯ ◯ ◯
◯ ◯ ◯ ◯ ◯ ◯ ◯

| WORKOUT | TIME | DURATION | CALORIES BURNED |
|---------|------|----------|-----------------|
| _____ | _____ | _____ | _____ |
| _____ | _____ | _____ | _____ |
| _____ | _____ | _____ | _____ |

WATER
(8-12 GLASSES PER DAY
◯ ◯ ◯ ◯ ◯ ◯ ◯
◯ ◯ ◯ ◯ ◯ ◯ ◯

| WORKOUT | TIME | DURATION | CALORIES BURNED |
|---------|------|----------|-----------------|
| _____ | _____ | _____ | _____ |
| _____ | _____ | _____ | _____ |
| _____ | _____ | _____ | _____ |

WATER
(8-12 GLASSES PER DAY
◯ ◯ ◯ ◯ ◯ ◯ ◯
◯ ◯ ◯ ◯ ◯ ◯ ◯

REMARKS:

# EXERCISE LOG

| DATE: | Su M Tu W Th F Sa |
|---|---|

| EXERCISES | SETS | TIME |
|---|---|---|
| | | |
| | | |
| | | |
| | | |
| | | |
| | | |
| | | |
| | | |
| | | |
| | | |
| | | |
| | | |
| | | |

# This Weeks

# Workout

- Record Your Weekly Workout

- Record Your Daily Workout

- Record Calories Burned

# DAILY LOG

| DATE: | | Su M Tu W Th F Sa | | |

| TIME | QTY | FOOD | CALORIES | FAT |
|------|-----|------|----------|-----|
| | | | | |
| | | | | |
| | | | | |
| | | | | |
| | | | | |
| | | | | |
| | | | | |
| | | | | |
| | | | | |
| | | | | |
| | | | | |
| | | | | |
| | | | | |
| | | | | |
| | | | | |
| | | | | |
| | | | | |
| | | | | |
| | | | | |
| | | | | |
| | | | | |
| | | | | |
| | | | | |
| | | | | |
| | | | | |

# WORK IT OUT

| WORKOUT | TIME | DURATION | CALORIES BURNED |
|---------|------|----------|-----------------|
| _____ | _____ | _____ | _____ |
| _____ | _____ | _____ | _____ |
| _____ | _____ | _____ | _____ |

WATER
(8-12 GLASSES PER DAY

◯ ◯ ◯ ◯ ◯ ◯ ◯
◯ ◯ ◯ ◯ ◯ ◯ ◯

| WORKOUT | TIME | DURATION | CALORIES BURNED |
|---------|------|----------|-----------------|
| _____ | _____ | _____ | _____ |
| _____ | _____ | _____ | _____ |
| _____ | _____ | _____ | _____ |

WATER
(8-12 GLASSES PER DAY

◯ ◯ ◯ ◯ ◯ ◯ ◯
◯ ◯ ◯ ◯ ◯ ◯ ◯

| WORKOUT | TIME | DURATION | CALORIES BURNED |
|---------|------|----------|-----------------|
| _____ | _____ | _____ | _____ |
| _____ | _____ | _____ | _____ |
| _____ | _____ | _____ | _____ |

WATER
(8-12 GLASSES PER DAY

◯ ◯ ◯ ◯ ◯ ◯ ◯
◯ ◯ ◯ ◯ ◯ ◯ ◯

REMARKS:

# WORK IT OUT

| WORKOUT | TIME | DURATION | CALORIES BURNED |
|---------|------|----------|-----------------|
| _____ | _____ | _____ | _____ |
| _____ | _____ | _____ | _____ |
| _____ | _____ | _____ | _____ |

WATER
(8-12 GLASSES PER DAY

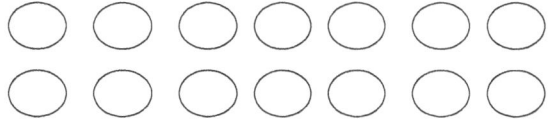

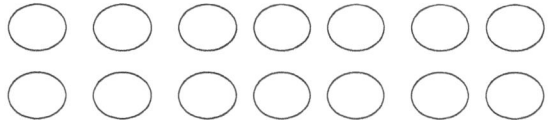

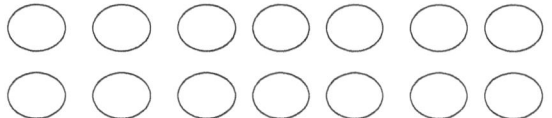

◯ ◯ ◯ ◯ ◯ ◯ ◯
◯ ◯ ◯ ◯ ◯ ◯ ◯

| WORKOUT | TIME | DURATION | CALORIES BURNED |
|---------|------|----------|-----------------|
| _____ | _____ | _____ | _____ |
| _____ | _____ | _____ | _____ |
| _____ | _____ | _____ | _____ |

WATER
(8-12 GLASSES PER DAY

◯ ◯ ◯ ◯ ◯ ◯ ◯
◯ ◯ ◯ ◯ ◯ ◯ ◯

| WORKOUT | TIME | DURATION | CALORIES BURNED |
|---------|------|----------|-----------------|
| _____ | _____ | _____ | _____ |
| _____ | _____ | _____ | _____ |
| _____ | _____ | _____ | _____ |

WATER
(8-12 GLASSES PER DAY

◯ ◯ ◯ ◯ ◯ ◯ ◯
◯ ◯ ◯ ◯ ◯ ◯ ◯

REMARKS:

# WORK IT OUT

| WORKOUT | TIME | DURATION | CALORIES BURNED |
|---|---|---|---|
| _____ | _____ | _____ | _____ |
| _____ | _____ | _____ | _____ |
| _____ | _____ | _____ | _____ |

WATER
(8-12 GLASSES PER DAY

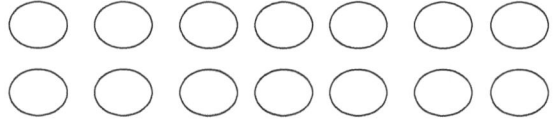

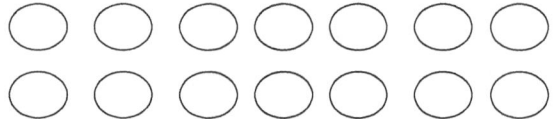

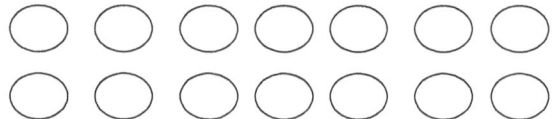

◯ ◯ ◯ ◯ ◯ ◯ ◯
◯ ◯ ◯ ◯ ◯ ◯ ◯

| WORKOUT | TIME | DURATION | CALORIES BURNED |
|---|---|---|---|
| _____ | _____ | _____ | _____ |
| _____ | _____ | _____ | _____ |

WATER
(8-12 GLASSES PER DAY

◯ ◯ ◯ ◯ ◯ ◯ ◯
◯ ◯ ◯ ◯ ◯ ◯ ◯

| WORKOUT | TIME | DURATION | CALORIES BURNED |
|---|---|---|---|
| _____ | _____ | _____ | _____ |
| _____ | _____ | _____ | _____ |

WATER
(8-12 GLASSES PER DAY

◯ ◯ ◯ ◯ ◯ ◯ ◯
◯ ◯ ◯ ◯ ◯ ◯ ◯

REMARKS:

# WORK IT OUT

| WORKOUT | TIME | DURATION | CALORIES BURNED |
|---------|------|----------|-----------------|
| _____ | _____ | _____ | _____ |
| _____ | _____ | _____ | _____ |
| _____ | _____ | _____ | _____ |

WATER
(8-12 GLASSES PER DAY

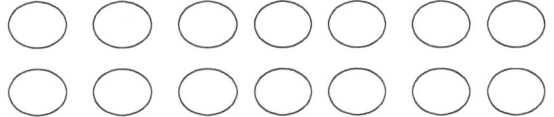

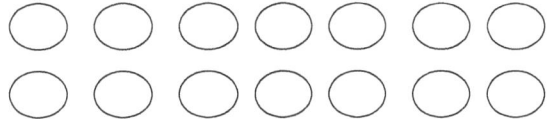

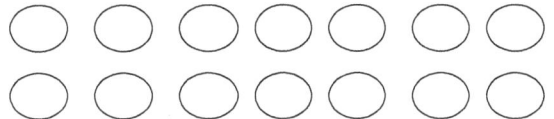

◯ ◯ ◯ ◯ ◯ ◯ ◯
◯ ◯ ◯ ◯ ◯ ◯ ◯

| WORKOUT | TIME | DURATION | CALORIES BURNED |
|---------|------|----------|-----------------|
| _____ | _____ | _____ | _____ |
| _____ | _____ | _____ | _____ |
| _____ | _____ | _____ | _____ |

WATER
(8-12 GLASSES PER DAY

◯ ◯ ◯ ◯ ◯ ◯ ◯
◯ ◯ ◯ ◯ ◯ ◯ ◯

| WORKOUT | TIME | DURATION | CALORIES BURNED |
|---------|------|----------|-----------------|
| _____ | _____ | _____ | _____ |
| _____ | _____ | _____ | _____ |
| _____ | _____ | _____ | _____ |

WATER
(8-12 GLASSES PER DAY

◯ ◯ ◯ ◯ ◯ ◯ ◯
◯ ◯ ◯ ◯ ◯ ◯ ◯

REMARKS:

# WORK IT OUT

| WORKOUT | TIME | DURATION | CALORIES BURNED |
|---|---|---|---|
| _____ | _____ | _____ | _____ |
| _____ | _____ | _____ | _____ |
| _____ | _____ | _____ | _____ |

WATER
(8-12 GLASSES PER DAY    ◯ ◯ ◯ ◯ ◯ ◯ ◯
◯ ◯ ◯ ◯ ◯ ◯ ◯

| WORKOUT | TIME | DURATION | CALORIES BURNED |
|---|---|---|---|
| _____ | _____ | _____ | _____ |
| _____ | _____ | _____ | _____ |
| _____ | _____ | _____ | _____ |

WATER
(8-12 GLASSES PER DAY    ◯ ◯ ◯ ◯ ◯ ◯ ◯
◯ ◯ ◯ ◯ ◯ ◯ ◯

| WORKOUT | TIME | DURATION | CALORIES BURNED |
|---|---|---|---|
| _____ | _____ | _____ | _____ |
| _____ | _____ | _____ | _____ |
| _____ | _____ | _____ | _____ |

WATER
(8-12 GLASSES PER DAY    ◯ ◯ ◯ ◯ ◯ ◯ ◯
◯ ◯ ◯ ◯ ◯ ◯ ◯

REMARKS:

# WORK IT OUT

| WORKOUT | TIME | DURATION | CALORIES BURNED |
|---------|------|----------|-----------------|
| _____ | _____ | _____ | _____ |
| _____ | _____ | _____ | _____ |
| _____ | _____ | _____ | _____ |

WATER
(8-12 GLASSES PER DAY

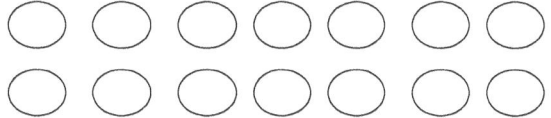

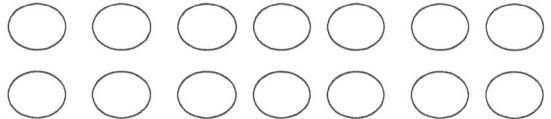

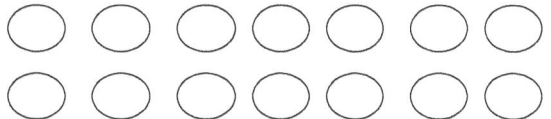

◯ ◯ ◯ ◯ ◯ ◯ ◯
◯ ◯ ◯ ◯ ◯ ◯ ◯

| WORKOUT | TIME | DURATION | CALORIES BURNED |
|---------|------|----------|-----------------|
| _____ | _____ | _____ | _____ |
| _____ | _____ | _____ | _____ |
| _____ | _____ | _____ | _____ |

WATER
(8-12 GLASSES PER DAY

◯ ◯ ◯ ◯ ◯ ◯ ◯
◯ ◯ ◯ ◯ ◯ ◯ ◯

| WORKOUT | TIME | DURATION | CALORIES BURNED |
|---------|------|----------|-----------------|
| _____ | _____ | _____ | _____ |
| _____ | _____ | _____ | _____ |
| _____ | _____ | _____ | _____ |

WATER
(8-12 GLASSES PER DAY

◯ ◯ ◯ ◯ ◯ ◯ ◯
◯ ◯ ◯ ◯ ◯ ◯ ◯

REMARKS:

# EXERCISE LOG

| DATE: | Su M Tu W Th F Sa |
|---|---|

| EXERCISES | SETS | TIME |
|---|---|---|
|  |  |  |
|  |  |  |
|  |  |  |
|  |  |  |
|  |  |  |
|  |  |  |
|  |  |  |
|  |  |  |
|  |  |  |
|  |  |  |
|  |  |  |
|  |  |  |
|  |  |  |

# This Weeks

# Workout

- Record Your Weekly Workout

- Record Your Daily Workout

- Record Calories Burned

# DAILY LOG

| DATE: | Su M Tu W Th F Sa | | | |
|---|---|---|---|---|
| TIME | QTY | FOOD | CALORIES | FAT |
|  |  |  |  |  |
|  |  |  |  |  |
|  |  |  |  |  |
|  |  |  |  |  |
|  |  |  |  |  |
|  |  |  |  |  |
|  |  |  |  |  |
|  |  |  |  |  |
|  |  |  |  |  |
|  |  |  |  |  |
|  |  |  |  |  |
|  |  |  |  |  |
|  |  |  |  |  |
|  |  |  |  |  |
|  |  |  |  |  |
|  |  |  |  |  |
|  |  |  |  |  |
|  |  |  |  |  |
|  |  |  |  |  |
|  |  |  |  |  |
|  |  |  |  |  |
|  |  |  |  |  |
|  |  |  |  |  |
|  |  |  |  |  |
|  |  |  |  |  |
|  |  |  |  |  |

# WORK IT OUT

| WORKOUT | TIME | DURATION | CALORIES BURNED |
|---------|------|----------|-----------------|
| _____ | _____ | _____ | _____ |
| _____ | _____ | _____ | _____ |
| _____ | _____ | _____ | _____ |

WATER
(8-12 GLASSES PER DAY    ◯ ◯ ◯ ◯ ◯ ◯ ◯
◯ ◯ ◯ ◯ ◯ ◯ ◯

| WORKOUT | TIME | DURATION | CALORIES BURNED |
|---------|------|----------|-----------------|
| _____ | _____ | _____ | _____ |
| _____ | _____ | _____ | _____ |
| _____ | _____ | _____ | _____ |

WATER
(8-12 GLASSES PER DAY    ◯ ◯ ◯ ◯ ◯ ◯ ◯
◯ ◯ ◯ ◯ ◯ ◯ ◯

| WORKOUT | TIME | DURATION | CALORIES BURNED |
|---------|------|----------|-----------------|
| _____ | _____ | _____ | _____ |
| _____ | _____ | _____ | _____ |
| _____ | _____ | _____ | _____ |

WATER
(8-12 GLASSES PER DAY    ◯ ◯ ◯ ◯ ◯ ◯ ◯
◯ ◯ ◯ ◯ ◯ ◯ ◯

REMARKS:

# WORK IT OUT

| WORKOUT | TIME | DURATION | CALORIES BURNED |
|---------|------|----------|-----------------|
| _____ | _____ | _____ | _____ |
| _____ | _____ | _____ | _____ |
| _____ | _____ | _____ | _____ |

WATER
(8-12 GLASSES PER DAY    ◯ ◯ ◯ ◯ ◯ ◯ ◯
◯ ◯ ◯ ◯ ◯ ◯ ◯

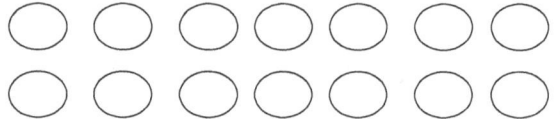

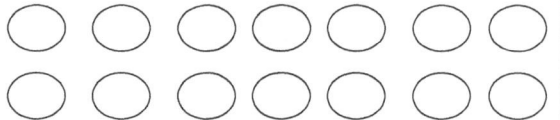

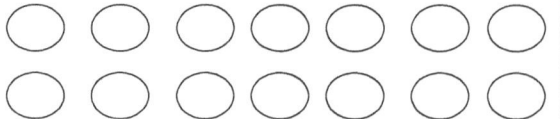

| WORKOUT | TIME | DURATION | CALORIES BURNED |
|---------|------|----------|-----------------|
| _____ | _____ | _____ | _____ |
| _____ | _____ | _____ | _____ |
| _____ | _____ | _____ | _____ |

WATER
(8-12 GLASSES PER DAY    ◯ ◯ ◯ ◯ ◯ ◯ ◯
◯ ◯ ◯ ◯ ◯ ◯ ◯

| WORKOUT | TIME | DURATION | CALORIES BURNED |
|---------|------|----------|-----------------|
| _____ | _____ | _____ | _____ |
| _____ | _____ | _____ | _____ |
| _____ | _____ | _____ | _____ |

WATER
(8-12 GLASSES PER DAY    ◯ ◯ ◯ ◯ ◯ ◯ ◯
◯ ◯ ◯ ◯ ◯ ◯ ◯

REMARKS:

# WORK IT OUT

| WORKOUT | TIME | DURATION | CALORIES BURNED |
|---------|------|----------|-----------------|
| _____ | _____ | _____ | _____ |
| _____ | _____ | _____ | _____ |
| _____ | _____ | | |

WATER
(8-12 GLASSES PER DAY

◯ ◯ ◯ ◯ ◯ ◯ ◯
◯ ◯ ◯ ◯ ◯ ◯ ◯

| WORKOUT | TIME | DURATION | CALORIES BURNED |
|---------|------|----------|-----------------|
| _____ | _____ | _____ | _____ |
| _____ | _____ | _____ | _____ |
| _____ | _____ | | |

WATER
(8-12 GLASSES PER DAY

◯ ◯ ◯ ◯ ◯ ◯ ◯
◯ ◯ ◯ ◯ ◯ ◯ ◯

| WORKOUT | TIME | DURATION | CALORIES BURNED |
|---------|------|----------|-----------------|
| _____ | _____ | _____ | _____ |
| _____ | _____ | _____ | _____ |
| _____ | _____ | | |

WATER
(8-12 GLASSES PER DAY

◯ ◯ ◯ ◯ ◯ ◯ ◯
◯ ◯ ◯ ◯ ◯ ◯ ◯

REMARKS:

# WORK IT OUT

| WORKOUT | TIME | DURATION | CALORIES BURNED |
|---|---|---|---|
| _____ | _____ | _____ | _____ |
| _____ | _____ | _____ | _____ |
| _____ | _____ | _____ | _____ |

WATER
(8-12 GLASSES PER DAY

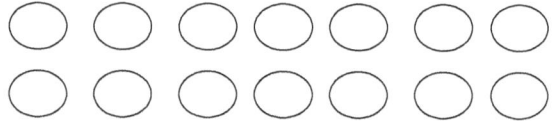

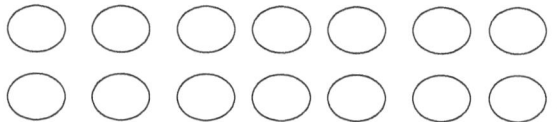

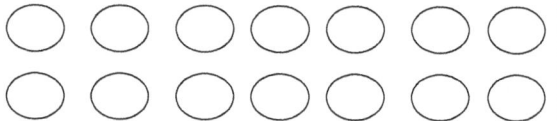

◯ ◯ ◯ ◯ ◯ ◯ ◯
◯ ◯ ◯ ◯ ◯ ◯ ◯

| WORKOUT | TIME | DURATION | CALORIES BURNED |
|---|---|---|---|
| _____ | _____ | _____ | _____ |
| _____ | _____ | _____ | _____ |
| _____ | _____ | _____ | _____ |

WATER
(8-12 GLASSES PER DAY

◯ ◯ ◯ ◯ ◯ ◯ ◯
◯ ◯ ◯ ◯ ◯ ◯ ◯

| WORKOUT | TIME | DURATION | CALORIES BURNED |
|---|---|---|---|
| _____ | _____ | _____ | _____ |
| _____ | _____ | _____ | _____ |
| _____ | _____ | _____ | _____ |

WATER
(8-12 GLASSES PER DAY

◯ ◯ ◯ ◯ ◯ ◯ ◯
◯ ◯ ◯ ◯ ◯ ◯ ◯

REMARKS:

# WORK IT OUT

| WORKOUT | TIME | DURATION | CALORIES BURNED |
|---------|------|----------|-----------------|
| _____ | _____ | _____ | _____ |
| _____ | _____ | _____ | _____ |
| _____ | _____ | _____ | _____ |

WATER
(8-12 GLASSES PER DAY

◯ ◯ ◯ ◯ ◯ ◯ ◯
◯ ◯ ◯ ◯ ◯ ◯ ◯

| WORKOUT | TIME | DURATION | CALORIES BURNED |
|---------|------|----------|-----------------|
| _____ | _____ | _____ | _____ |
| _____ | _____ | _____ | _____ |
| _____ | _____ | _____ | _____ |

WATER
(8-12 GLASSES PER DAY

◯ ◯ ◯ ◯ ◯ ◯ ◯
◯ ◯ ◯ ◯ ◯ ◯ ◯

| WORKOUT | TIME | DURATION | CALORIES BURNED |
|---------|------|----------|-----------------|
| _____ | _____ | _____ | _____ |
| _____ | _____ | _____ | _____ |
| _____ | _____ | _____ | _____ |

WATER
(8-12 GLASSES PER DAY

◯ ◯ ◯ ◯ ◯ ◯ ◯
◯ ◯ ◯ ◯ ◯ ◯ ◯

REMARKS:

# WORK IT OUT

| WORKOUT | TIME | DURATION | CALORIES BURNED |
|---------|------|----------|-----------------|
| _____ | _____ | _____ | _____ |
| _____ | _____ | _____ | _____ |
| _____ | _____ | _____ | _____ |

WATER
(8-12 GLASSES PER DAY

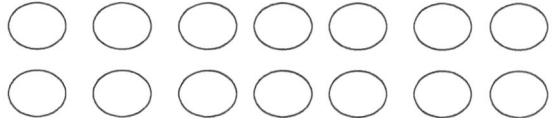

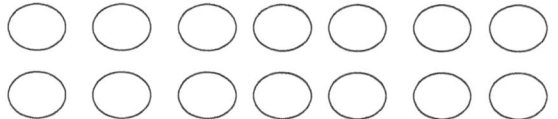

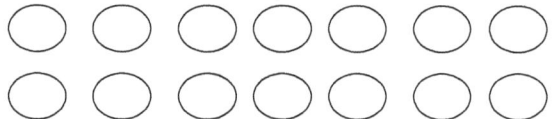

◯ ◯ ◯ ◯ ◯ ◯ ◯
◯ ◯ ◯ ◯ ◯ ◯ ◯

| WORKOUT | TIME | DURATION | CALORIES BURNED |
|---------|------|----------|-----------------|
| _____ | _____ | _____ | _____ |
| _____ | _____ | _____ | _____ |
| _____ | _____ | _____ | _____ |

WATER
(8-12 GLASSES PER DAY

◯ ◯ ◯ ◯ ◯ ◯ ◯
◯ ◯ ◯ ◯ ◯ ◯ ◯

| WORKOUT | TIME | DURATION | CALORIES BURNED |
|---------|------|----------|-----------------|
| _____ | _____ | _____ | _____ |
| _____ | _____ | _____ | _____ |
| _____ | _____ | _____ | _____ |

WATER
(8-12 GLASSES PER DAY

◯ ◯ ◯ ◯ ◯ ◯ ◯
◯ ◯ ◯ ◯ ◯ ◯ ◯

REMARKS:

# EXERCISE LOG

| DATE: | Su M Tu W Th F Sa |
|---|---|

| EXERCISES | SETS | TIME |
|---|---|---|
| | | |
| | | |
| | | |
| | | |
| | | |
| | | |
| | | |
| | | |
| | | |
| | | |
| | | |
| | | |
| | | |
| | | |